ESSAYS TOWARD
REALISTIC SYNTAX

LINGUISTICS RESEARCH
MONOGRAPH SERIES

Volume 1

Base Generated Syntax, M. K. Brame

Volume 2

Essays Toward Realistic Syntax, M. K. Brame

ESSAYS
TOWARD
REALISTIC SYNTAX

M. K. BRAME

NOIT AMROFER NA SEATTLE

'79

Noit Amrofer Publishing Co.
P. O. Box 15176
Seattle, Washington 98115

Library of Congress Card Number 79-67347
ISBN 0-932998-01-1

For my plant

CONTENTS

Introduction   9

Realistic Grammar   19

Chomsky/Lasnik Filters
Are Special Cases of Functional Deviance   67

The Opacity Condition,
The Nominative Island Condition,
And the Myth of Control   111

Quantifiers,
Reciprocals,
And Raising   131

The Base Hypothesis
And the Spelling Prohibition   151

Alternatives to the Tensed S
And Specified Subject Conditions   183

INTRODUCTION

More than two decades ago, Chomsky made the following remarks at the Third Texas Conference on Problems of Linguistic Analysis in English.

> Transformational rules are, of course, an important part of traditional grammar. E.g., O. Jespersen argues, on what we will reconstruct as transformational grounds, that "the doctor's arrival" is different in structure from "the man's house," despite superficial similarity, because of its relation to the sentence "the doctor arrives." This observation, which, I think, is entirely correct is criticized by E. A. Nida . . . as a "serious distortion and complication of the formal and functional values . . ."

A decade later, in "Remarks on Nominalization," we find that the "superficial similarity" between *the doctor's arrival* and *the man's house* might not be so superficial after all. Poor Jespersen's "entirely correct" transformational analysis can now be reconstructed according to the latest line, presumably. At any rate, the move to the surface had begun.

The essays collected in this volume are ripples set in motion by the stone cast into the quiet pool of transformational grammar of the '60s. They are, in some measure, a reaction to work which fails to carry the move to the surface to its logical limit and to recognize the lexicon as the locus of syntactic distributional generalizations. Seen in broader perspective, they are a natural outgrowth of Chomsky's flirtation with the lexicon in *Aspects of the Theory of Syntax* and "Remarks on Nominalization". They are my own stepping stones to a vantage point which those who cling to transformations and conditions and constraints and filters will continue to resist.

My first negative reaction to transformational grammar was inspired by a reading of an introduction to syntax by Roberts in 1964. Roberts, having learned of transformational grammar, wrote a programmed course in which he provided an orthodox approach to infinitival complements. This analysis struck me as somewhat contrived at the time. My reaction, then, as it is now, was one of discomfort and reluctance to accept the alleged motivation for the abstract analysis.

9

Upon entering MIT as a graduate student in 1966, I, like so many others, was subjected to the party line on abstract subjects and Equi. Although I soon fell into the rhythm of MIT factory life, and even came under the influence of generative semanticists, who taught me introductory syntax, I continued to harbour lingering doubts about the whole question of Equi and abstract subjects. But preoccupation with phonology and teaching did not allow time to explore my heretical ideas, so it was not until 1972, in preparation for my Fulbright-Hays lectures in Holland, that I began to reassess transformational syntax with some systematicity. My thoughts of the period are recorded as Part II of *Conjectures and Refutations in Syntax and Semantics* (hereafter CRSS).

Besides the work of Chomsky, mentioned above, I can clearly discern three related, though quite distinct, influences on my thinking. Emonds, more than anyone else, provided the most convincing demonstration of the importance of phrase structure at a time when transformations were the focus of attention. Rosenbaum's dissertation had served as an impetus for work on complex sentences in English, and as a consequence, up until Emonds, transformations were the rage. Although I later took issue with Emonds' structure-preserving hypothesis, cf. CRSS, I still feel that his work, which culminated in his dissertation *Root and Structure-Preserving Transformations*, had an enormous influence on much subsequent work; this influence is seldom acknowledged today, nor is it common knowledge that Emonds adopted as early as 1968 an analysis of passives as base generated structures and suggested an analysis of infinitival complements without abstract subjects, cf. CRSS, p. 144, fn. 7. But influences were such that these analyses, so far ahead of their time (still unrecognized by trace theorists), were abandoned in his dissertation proper.

A second influence derived from my own work in phonology. I had come to the conclusion during the course of my work on Maltese in '68 that subject pronoun prefixes must be provided in the lexicon and that these prefixes should be combined by lexical rules with their associated stems prior to lexical insertion. How else could it be explained that subject pronouns were analyzed in terms of the initial cycle to account for the interaction of stress and segmental processes? Publication of my work on Maltese was delayed until I had the opportunity to confirm the data with native speakers in Malta during the summer of 1970. My work on Maltese finally appeared in *Contributions to Generative Phonology* in '72. In the published paper, evidence is provided for treating the subject pronoun prefixes as analyzed during the course of the initial cycle; however, the lexical rules of combination which juxtapose the prefixes and stems were not provided. In fact, it was not until '78 that I returned to this topic and realized the full implications of this omission—that phonological rules, like transformations, really should not alter words, stems, or affixes, but should instead serve as instructions for the proper combination of the full range of phonetic alternants, or alternatively, as filters on their proper juxtaposition. This work was cited as "Lexical Phonology" in Yildirim's dissertation, *A Functional Interpretive Approach to Turkish*, although the paper was completed only recently. Yildirim's dissertation and Guerssel's work are much in the spirit of this conception, although both have contributed their own important insights, analyses, and proposals.

The realization that phonological rules should not alter words, mentioned above, can be viewed as a generalization of the Spelling Prohibition, which was proposed in "The Base Hypothesis and the Spelling Prohibition". This article appeared in *Linguistic Analysis*. It is reprinted here as the second to last essay.

A further influence of my work in phonology on my thinking in syntax concerns research on Arabic phonology. I had discovered an extremely complex set of relations between the so-called weak stems of Arabic, including hollow stems, doubled stems, and what I called lame stems. The generalization was not adequately expressed in my dissertation on Arabic phonology, but I soon discovered a means of capturing the generalization after submission, defence, and acceptance of the original. Part of a seminar at the University of Washington during the spring of 1971 was devoted to this topic, and I also lectured on the same material in Utrecht in '73–'74. Expressing the generalization entailed positing an intermediate representation as the optimal underlying representation, together with two sets of rules, one mapping the optimal representations onto superficial representations and one mapping them onto abstract representations, a view not incompatible with traditional phonemics of the structuralists, though differing in many respects. This work was delivered with handouts as "Interpretive Phonology" at C. L. Baker's conference at the University of Texas during the spring of '72. It was never published; related, though somewhat different, ideas have subsequently been developed quite independently by Eliasson in Sweden and Leben and Robinson at Stanford. Around 1978, I was to see that the generalization is best expressed within a framework of lexical phonology. If one compares the outlines of the analysis presented as "Interpretive Phonology", I think one will see its relation to the syntactic analyses provided in CRSS.

In addition to the aforementioned influences, I should not fail to mention Bresnan's sparkling paper "Sentence Stress and Syntactic Transformations", published in *Language* in 1971. Although this paper dealt for the most part with stress and related phenomena, it was the almost casual remarks on VP which attracted my attention and rekindled my interest in this topic. In her paper, Bresnan argued that Object Shift (=Tough

Movement) constructions, which I have subsequently called scopal predicate constructions, should be analyzed in terms of VP. It is wrong to assume an abstract S or S̄ with concomitant abstract subject. Upon reading this paper, memories of my dissatisfaction with Equi were awakened, and I immediately saw that the VP-hypothesis should be extended to all infinitival constructions. This step, in turn, had serious consequences for transformational grammar and, therefore, it is understandable that those bent on retaining transformations should ignore these consequences and fail to explore the uncharted terrain. The consequences were recorded in my "A Reanalysis of a Class of Transformations," cited in my "On the Abstractness of Syntactic Structure: The VP Controversy", the latter appearing in *Linguistic Analysis*, several years after having been solicited, and then rejected, for the Benveniste festschrift. The former article I sent to Bresnan in '74 and I believe it had some influence on her later thinking. It was ultimately published as Chapter 5 of CRSS under a different title.

While in Holland I attempted to formulate a complete range of unbounded transformations as lexical redundancy rules; however, I abandoned this attempt, mistakenly it seems, for stupid reasons, adopting instead an "inverse" treatment, as laid out in CRSS. Although the analyses provided in CRSS are breathlessly quick and lacking in detail, I think one can discern, nevertheless, a series of steps in the right direction, bridged by later work. One can, for example, find an attempt to generalize a range of unbounded constructions as a single rule of COMP-Insertion and a discussion of the generalized filtering problem. This work antedates Chomsky's own attempt at generalizing the full range of unbounded transformations. It was sent to him in 1974 and he was kind enough to provide extensive comments. I have not failed to notice, however, that Chomsky has repeatedly cited my critique of generative semantics favorably while consistently omitting discussion of Part II, which has implications for his own theoretical perspective.

During my tenure at Utrecht, Chomsky's "Conditions on Transformations" was a central topic of discussion by the local inmates of the Instituut. Their enthusiasm I failed to share, for I disagreed with the basic assumptions underlying this work. In the article, Chomsky referred to Bresnan's "Sentence Stress and Syntactic Transformations", noting that "her proposal is to take the bracketed expressions as VPs, an approach which . . . has far-reaching effects on the formulation of many rules" [p. 265]. How could such far-reaching consequences be dismissed without serious discussion? It was clear to me that the consequences were even more serious than intimated, since an extended VP-hypothesis gave the lie to a full range of transformations, and, hence, a fortiori, to the conditions on transformations that Chomsky had proposed.

My disapproval of this approach was given expression in "Alternatives to the Tensed S and Specified Subject Conditions", which was delivered during the course of a seminar at the University of Washington during the fall of 1975. It was published in *Linguistics and Philosophy* two years later and brings up the rear of the selection offered in this volume. Although significant progress has been made since the appearance of this article, I think a good deal of the criticism leveled against the constraints approach ring true today.

Chomsky and Lasnik pursued the theory which had originated in "Conditions on Transformations" in their article "Filters and Control", which appeared in *Linguistic Inquiry*. Here they extended the theory to include a wide range of ad hoc filters with no appreciable formal analysis of control. My response to this work is provided in the second essay of this collection, "Chomsky/Lasnik Filters Are Special Cases of Functional Deviance". A fragment of this paper was delivered at the Sloan Workshop at Stanford in January of this year (1979) with Chomsky and Lasnik in attendance. A hint of Chomsky's response to my presentation is provided in the initial essay of this collection, "Realistic Grammar", which was delivered at the Conference on Current Approaches to Syntax in Milwaukee, Wisconsin during March of this year. This paper I originally submitted to *Linguistic Inquiry* where it was rejected.

One of the papers offered here deals with Chomsky's latest paper "On Binding". It shows, I believe, that his latest revisions and refinements of trace theory offer no real improvement over his original conditions. All lead to significant loss of generalization and suffer from a failure to recognize the integrity of lexical items. Here, for perhaps the first time, one begins to perceive an affinity of his work with that of generative semantics. Abstract case is introduced without a single explicit provision for the actual treatment of lexical items. The formal account of the actual content of words is taken to be mere detail, a trait of generative semantics in its heyday, cf. Part I of CRSS. As time now runs out on trace theory, one sees ever more far-fetched devices proposed to accommodate counterexamples that genuinely follow from more realistic approaches. Just as generative semanticists were inspired to propose global rules and other prophylactic devices to immunize their theory against refutation, so also trace theorists have begun to follow suit by adopting theoretical constructs which are seldom made explicit. It is now impossible to evaluate claims relating to the mystical level of logical form, for lack of explicitness, and Chomsky more recently has even proposed a generative semantics-like analysis of examples such as *John struck me as like Harry* and *John regards me as like Harry*, cf. "On Binding".

The articles collected here are, with two exceptions, compiled in reverse chronological order. The piece critical of "On Binding" was presented during the spring quarter of this year at a seminar at the University of Washington. It seemed more appropriate following the articles "Realistic Grammar" and "Chomsky/Lasnik Filters Are Special Cases of Functional Deviance", although the latter antedate it. The paper entitled "Quantifiers, Reciprocals, and Raising" was actually composed prior to the final two essays and is cited in the concluding paper. But since this paper has not previously appeared in print, it has been placed out of chronological sequence, before the two essays which are reprinted here. My original intention was to extensively rework this article, but too much time has elapsed and my interest has waned; there are a number of points in this paper, nevertheless, which are still worthy of consideration; so I include it here as the third to last essay.

Lest I convey the impression that I consider the approach offered here as anything definitive, let me hasten to emphasize that ideas continue to evolve; as always, there are many alternative ways of formulating binding, anaphora, and other processes of interest in these papers. Whatever the final outcome of the precise form which the best theory will assume in the future, I am laying odds that it will be a theory which accords with that presented here in at least the following respects.

i. Abstract subjects or PRO (or $[e]_{NP}$, etc.) along with the accompanying abstract S or $\bar{S}$ will play no role. Infinitival complements will be analyzed as infinitival complements, i.e. some version of $\overline{VP}$.

ii. Transformations in the sense of the standard theory, extended standard theory, or trace theory will play no role. There will come a time when linguists agree that transformations do not exist.

iii. Conditions, constraints, metaconditions, or metaconstraints such as the Specified Subject Condition, Propositional Island Constraint, Opacity Condition, Tensed S Condition, Nominal Island Constraint, Subjacency, A/A Principle, Relativized A/A, Recoverability of Deletion, etc. will play absolutely no role. There will come a time when linguists agree that the effects of such conditions follow from more lexically based theories.

iv. Lexical items will not be altered by transformations, nor, even by phonological rules. There will come a time when linguists agree that words are not to be abused by case marking rules and other ad hoc processes.

These pronouncements may seem bold at this stage of our understanding, but these are the objectives toward which my own research has been channeled in recent years. Of interest for serious minded syntacticians will be a comparison of alternative theories which do not incorporate transformations, while satisfying the desiderata of (i)–(iv). Perhaps these essays can provide some stimulus towards this end, an interesting and intriguing prospect for the '80s.

REALISTIC GRAMMAR

Sensei, do these facts really follow?

> *John, who I wanted to see and who I did see, is my friend.*
> **John, who I wanted to see and who I did, is my friend.*
> *They say John is eating beans, which he is.*
>
> *John is eating beans.*
> *Who is?*
> **What is he?*

Yes, gakusei, read on.

Introductory Remarks

1. Linguistic Problems
    1.1 Binding
    1.2 The Multiple Ambiguity Problem
    1.3 The Problem of Generalizing Anaphora
    1.4 Interaction of Binding and Ellipsis

2. A Sketch of the Theory

3. Tentative Solutions
    3.1 Binding
    3.2 VP-Ellipsis
    3.3 Pronominalization and Ellipsis as Anaphora
    3.4 Binding and Anaphora

4. Conclusion
    4.1 Apparent Arguments Against Pure Interpretive Theories
    4.2 Nonexistence of Empty Nodes and Traces
    4.3 The Missing Argument Phenomenon
    4.4 Chomsky/Lasnik Filters
    4.5 Nonexistence of Ordering
    4.6 New Frontiers: Realistic Phonology
    4.7 Linguistic Problems

Notes

References

REALISTIC GRAMMAR*

Discussion of goals of syntax and linguistic theory will probably never amount to much. I have yet to see anything profound emerge from debates over introspection vs. techniques of elicitation, competence vs. performance, mentalism vs. antimentalism, and other high-level theoretical oppositions. My perspective is to let such topics lie and to turn to the really exciting domain of activity which I will characterize as *linguistic problems*. My view is that the ultimate fate of any theory of natural language will be determined not so much by metatheoretical arguments for it as by its ability to deal with the significant linguistic problems in a revealing manner, by its success in bringing together apparently disparate sets of facts and in providing explanations for apparent irregularities. There are a number of linguistic problems which have crystallized over the past decade or so of research within the framework of transformational grammar and it is to these problems that theoretically minded linguists should be devoting their energies.

In harmony with this view, I therefore wish to focus on several of these problems in my talk. I consider these problems to be central to the evaluation of any theory. They must ultimately be confronted regardless of theoretical bias.

The plan of my talk is the following: First, I will lay out four problems which I have chosen as representative of significant linguistic problems. Next I will provide a sketch of the theory I wish to advocate. Then I will offer solutions to these problems within the proposed framework. Finally, I wish to conclude by contrasting the proposed theory with trace theory.

1. LINGUISTIC PROBLEMS

What I consider to be the most significant problems of linguistic theory are outlined and developed in some detail in Brame (to appear a). In what

*This paper was presented at the Conference on Current Approaches to Syntax, Milwaukee, Wisconsin in March 1979.

19

follows, I have selected four of these problems as central to the syntax of English.

1.1 *Binding*

The question of binding is one which provides a challenge to any lingustic theory. Syntactic structures in English that exhibit binding include questions, relative clauses, focus constructions, topic structures, and comparative clauses, as illustrated below.

(1) a. What did Mary put into the garage?
     b. the car which Mary put into the garage
     c. It was the car that Mary put into the garage.
     d. This car Mary put into the garage.
     e. more cars than Mary put into the garage

A number of properties seem to suggest that these different construction types should be treated in a general way. For example, as is well-known, all exhibit a kind of deviance when two such constructions interact in a crucial way. Relevant examples illustrating this deviance include the following.

(2) X-question

     a. *Where did she ask which car Bill put __ __?   *question-question*
     b. *the girl who John asked the boy who hit __   *rel-question*
     c. *It was in the garage that she asked which car Bill put __ __.   *foc-question*
     d. *That car she asked where Bill put __ __.   *top-question*
     e. *John drank fewer beers than Mary asked who ate __ apples.   *com-question*
        cf. John drank fewer beers than Mary ate __ apples.

(3) X-rel

     a. *Which car did she see the boy who put __ into the garage?   *question-rel*
     b. *the boy who Mary likes the girl who hit __   *rel-rel*
     c. *It was this car that she saw the girl who drove __.   *foc-rel*
     d. *This car she saw the girl who drove __.   *top-rel*
     e. *John drank fewer beers than the boy who ate __ apples left.   *com-rel*

(4) X-foc

    a. *Which car was it in the garage that Mary put __ __? *question-foc*

    b. *the car which it was in the garage that Mary put __ __ *rel-foc*

    c. *It was the car that it was in the garage that Mary put __ __. *foc-foc*

    d. *This car it was in the garage that Mary put __ __. *top-foc*

    e. *John drank fewer beers than it was Mary that ate __ apples. *com-foc*

(5) X-top

    a. *Where did this car John put __ __? *question-top*

    b. *the garage into which this car John put __ __ *rel-top*

    c. *It was into this garage that this car John put __ __. *foc-top*

    d. *Into this garage this car John put __ __. *top-top*

    e. *John rode fewer bikes than into the garage Mary put __ cars __. *com-top*

(6) X-com

    a. *Who does John like Bill more than Sue likes __ __? *question-com*

    b. *the boy who John likes Bill more than Sue likes __ __ *rel-com*

    c. *This boy John likes Bill more than Sue likes __ __. *top-com*

    d. *It was this boy that John likes Bill more than Sue likes __ __. *foc-com*

    e. *I have more apples than John saw fewer girls than __ boys eat __. *com-com*

Let us call the property which distinguishes all of these examples, the *accessible scope property*. It is clear that it is not the accessible scope property alone that accounts for the deviance of at least some of these examples. For example, there seem to be independent reasons for the deviance of the X-top examples, since topic constructions are not normally permitted in embedded contexts, cf. Emonds (1976).

(7) a. *I realize that this car John put __ into the garage.

    b. *Mary always says this car she puts __ into the garage.

Nevertheless, the *accessible scope property* will be crucial to a satisfactory account of the majority of examples listed in (2)–(6).

A second property which is invariant across the full range of constructions adduced above is a property which I have elsewhere called the *filtering property*. The filtering property is illustrated for the full range of constructions below.

(8)   a. *Who(m) did John see Mary?   *question*
      b. *the boy who(m) John saw Mary   *rel*
      c. *It was John that Harry saw Mary.   *foc*
      d. *This hat Mary saw John.   *top*
      e. *more boys than the girls   *com*

The fact that all of the above-cited constructions exhibit both the accessible scope property and the filtering property suggests that we are dealing here with a single phenomenon, which I will term *binding*. Several proposals have been advanced to express the underlying generalization and these will be touched on below in section 3.

The problem of binding, then, is to provide a general characterization of the accessible scope property and the filtering property while at the same time providing an analysis which generalizes across construction types. In addition, the analysis must be sufficiently general to cut across category types, since categories other than NP are often involved. Thus, in addition to NP-like heads, we encounter PP-like heads in the case of relative clauses, questions, focus constructions, and topic structures.[1]

(8)   a. Into which bottle did Mary put the coins?   *question*
      b. the bottle into which Mary put the coins   *rel*
      c. It was into this bottle that Mary put the coins. *foc*
      d. Into this bottle Mary put the coins.   *top*

We also find sentential heads, as illustrated in the following paradigm.

(9)   a. What did Mary claim?   *question*
      b. Mary left, which was surprising.   *rel*
      c. It was simply that John failed that Bill thought
         had frightened Harry.   *foc*
      d. That Mary left I believe surprised Harry.   *top*

Other categories as well figure in the binding framework and the complete range of permissible argument types should be subsumed under one general analysis. A general treatment is once again suggested by the fact that we encounter the accessible scope property and the filtering property in connection with such examples. For example, in connection with the sentential case, we find the following deviant examples.[2]

(10) a. *That Mary left Bill saw the boy who believes __ surprised Harry.
      b. *That Mary left Bill believes that Sue is smart surprised Harry.

In summary, the problem of binding is that of presenting an analysis meeting the following desiderata.

   i. The analysis must generalize across construction types, e.g. relative clauses, questions, focus constructions, topic structures, comparative clauses in English.
   ii. The analysis must generalize across category types where relevant, e.g. NP, PP, etc. in English.
   iii. The analysis must account for the accessible scope property in a general way.
   iv. The analysis must account for the filtering property in a general way.

It should be noted, in passing from this topic, that not all languages treat each of the aforementioned construction types as in instance of binding. Thus, languages exhibiting question particles typically do not reflect the binding property. For example, in Japanese the question is typically marked with the particle *ka*, not only in the case of yes/no questions, but also in the case of *wh*-questions.

(11) a. Mary-ga   sakana-o   tot-ta
         Mary subj.   fish obj.   catch past
         Mary caught   the fish.
      b. Mary-ga   sakana-o   tot-ta ka?
         Did Mary catch the fish?
(12) a. dare-ga   sakana-o   tot-ta ka?
         who subj.   fish obj.   catch past Q
         Who caught the fish?

If Japanese questions are not instances of binding, we should not expect to encounter the accessible scope property when binding constructions interact with questions. Apparent binding constructions in Japanese include the relative clause, topic construction and focus structure, which are illustrated below.

(13) a. Mary-ga   tot-ta   sakana   *rel*
           Mary subj   catch past fish
           the fish that Mary caught
      b. Sakana-wa   Mary-ga   tot-ta.   *top*
           fish top   Mary subj. catch past
           The fish Mary caught.
      c. Mary-ga   tot-ta no wa sakana   da.   *foc*
           Mary subj   catch past nom fish   is
           It was the fish that Mary caught.

There is no related accessible scope violation when questions interact with relative clauses, focus constructions, and topic structures, as illustrated below.

(14) a. Mary-ga dare-ga   tot-ta ka to tazuneta sakana *rel-question*
        Mary subj who subj catch past Q comp asked   fish
        *the fish that Mary asked who caught
     b. Sono sakana-wa Mary-ga dare-ga   tot-ta   ka   to   tazuneta *top-question*
        that fish top   Mary subj who subj catch past Q comp asked
        *That fish Mary asked who caught.
     c. Mary-ga dare-ga   tot-ta ka to tazuneta no wa sono sakana da *foc-que*
        Mary subj who subj catch past Q comp asked   nom top that fish   is
        *It was that fish that Mary asked who caught.

Other interactions, however, do yield the accessible scope property of deviance.

(15) a. *Mary-wa tot-ta sakana.   top-rel
          Mary   the fish that __ caught
      b. *Mary-wa tot-ta no wa sakana da.   top-foc
          Mary, it was the fish that __ caught __.

It is interesting to note that there are examples illustrating the filtering property which correspond to the apparent binding constructions, although there is no such example corresponding to the question in Japanese.

(16) a. *Mary-ga booru-o   tot-ta   sakana
      *the fish that Mary caught the ball
   b. *Sakana-wa Mary-ga booru-o   tot-ta.   *top*
      *The fish Mary caught the ball.
   c. *Mary-ga booru-o tot-ta   no wa   sakana da. *foc*
      *It was the fish that Mary caught the ball.

Perhaps it is a property of all binding constructions that they exhibit apparent "holes" in their syntax. Thus, for example, when we compare the relative clause *Mary-ga tot-ta* with the sentence *Mary-ga sakana-o tot-ta*, we see that the former exhibits a hole, just as in English we find a hole in the relative clause *who John saw*. The same is true of the focus construction in Japanese, e.g. (13c). It does not hold for the question in Japanese, however, as contrasted with English.

If it is true that a structure must exhibit a hole to qualify as a binding construction, we might then expect that constructions exhibiting the resumptive pronoun phenomenon do not involve binding. There are many languages that include such constructions. Many apparently do not exhibit the accessible scope property, indicating that we are not dealing with binding, but many apparently do. Clearly, binding across languages is a topic which invites detailed research; it would be premature to simply write off the resumptive pronoun constructions as instances of "predication" or some other phenomenon. At the same time, it is not clear that they are genuine instances of binding. For some discussion, cf. Brame (1979a).

1.2 *The Multiple Ambiguity Problem*

Examples such as the following have been the focus of a good deal of activity within the transformational camp, cf. Wasow (1972) and Sag (1977).

(17) a. Mary has eaten kabsa and Bill has too.
   b. John is playing the oud and Hamza is too.

There is an interesting puzzle related to such constructions. Consider first the fact that the following examples are ambiguous.

(18) a. They are flying planes.
   b. This chicken is too hot to eat.
   c. She sees Harry more often than Sally.
   d. Tom looked up the pipe.

The ambiguity can be elucidated in terms of the following examples.

(19) a. They are flying these planes.
      b. They are those flying planes.
(20) a. This chicken is too hot for me to eat.
      b. This chicken is too hot to eat anything.
(21) a. She sees Harry more often than she sees Sally.
      b. She sees Harry more often than Sally sees him.
(22) a. Tom looked the pipe up in the catalogue.
      b. Tom looked way up the pipe.

Now a well-known puzzle arises in connection with the following examples.

(23) a. These are flying planes and those are too.
      b. This chicken is too hot to eat and that one is too.
      c. She sees Harry more often than Sally and Mary does too.
      d. Tom looked up the pipe and Sue did too.

Since the examples in the left conjunct are 2-ways ambiguous, one might have expected the resulting ellipsis cases to be 4-ways ambiguous, corresponding to the following four examples, taking (18a) as representative.

(24) a. These are [flying planes]$_{NP}$ and those are [flying planes]$_{NP}$ too.
      b. These are [flying planes]$_{VP}$ and those are [flying planes]$_{VP}$ too.
      c. These are [flying planes]$_{NP}$ and those are [flying planes]$_{VP}$ too.
      d. These are [flying planes]$_{VP}$ and those are [flying planes]$_{NP}$ too.

However, contrary to expectations, the examples in (23) are not 4-ways ambiguous; they are only 2-ways ambiguous. They exhibit only the parallel interpretations. Thus, again taking (18a) as representative, we see that it can have readings analogous to (24a) and (24b), but not to (24c) and (24d).

The *multiple ambiguity problem* [MAP] is that of accounting for the fact that examples such as those listed in (23) are not 4-ways ambiguous. The familiar transformational answer to this riddle is based on the notion of identity. If string identity is associated with deletion rules, then we would expect 4-way ambiguity under the assumption that the relevant examples are derived by means of a deletion rule. Because 4-way ambiguity is not observed, linguists have proposed stronger identity requirements and some have even gone so far as to propose global identity, cf. Chomsky (1968).

Any solution to MAP must be sufficiently general so as to extend to discourse. This conclusion follows from the observation that the same problem arises in connection with discourse, as illustrated below.

(25) a. These are flying planes.
      b. Those are too.

It is clear that this discourse is 2-ways ambiguous, not 4-ways ambiguous. Again, only the parallel interpretations are possible. A theory which is not sufficiently general to include coarser discourse relations will not succeed in providing a satisfying solution to MAP.

1.3 *The Problem of Generalizing Anaphora* [PGA]

For some time, it has been known that there is a generalization cutting across pronouns and ellipsis. Consider first the well-known paradigms involving pronouns.

(26) a. I saw *Bill* after Mary pointed *him* out to me.
      b. John thought *Mary* was tall when he saw *her*.
(27) a. *I saw *him* after Mary pointed *Bill* out to me.
      b. *John thought *she* was tall when he saw *Mary*.
(28) a. After Mary pointed *him* out to me, I saw *Bill*.
      b. When John saw *her*, he thought *Mary* was tall.

Example (27a) and example (27b) show that two NP's cannot be coindexed when the second is not a pronoun and the first commands the second. We find a similar state of affairs with ellipsis of the type discussed above in subsection 1.2.

(29) a. John has certainly tasted the beans if Bill has.
      b. Sally can't leave if Bill can't.
(30) a. *John has if Bill has tasted the beans.
      b. *Sally can't if Bill can't leave.
(31) a. If Bill has, then John has probably tasted the beans too.
      b. If Bill can't, then Sally can't leave either.

Examples (30a) and (30b) are deviant under the intended interpretation, just as (27a) and (27b) are deviant under the intended interpretation. (None of the examples is deviant, however, under a different interpretation where requisite antecedents are supplied.) Similar conditions hold between the verbal elements of (30) as hold between the pronouns of (27) with respect to command, precedence, and fully specified anaphor. Hence the deviance of the examples in both (27) and (30) should be expressed in a unified way.

If there is indeed a generalization to be expressed here, we might expect to find a similar distribution of data in discourse. This seems to be true. For example, the following parallelism seems to hold.

(32) a. John saw Bill.
      b. I saw him.
(33) a. John has eaten beans.
      b. I have too.
(34) a. John saw *him*.
      b. I saw *Bill* too.
(35) a. John has.
      b. I have *eaten beans too*.

In (32) and (33) we find that anaphora is well-formed in both cases. In (34) and (35) we find that anaphora is not possible. This suggests that a very similar phenomenon is being observed.[3]

The problem of anaphora, then, is to generalize pronouns and ellipsis so as to express the parallelism observed in terms of intrasentence and discourse relations.

1.4 *Interaction of Binding and Ellipsis*

The two processes discussed under subsection 1.1 and 1.3 converge to provide an extremely interesting problem. Consider the following discourses.

(36) a. John is eating beans.
      b. Who is?
(37) a. John is eating beans.
      b. *What is he?

In (36) we see that the subject of (a) can be questioned and that ellipsis is simultaneously permitted. By contrast, this is not so in (37) when the object is questioned. These observations hold, of course, for other forms of the auxiliary, including *have*, modals, *do*, and infinitival *to*. What underlies this distinction? The interaction problem is that of providing an analysis which yields insight into this question.

There are many other puzzles of interaction, cf. the examples on the main title page. Several of these will be discussed below in section 3.4.

2. A SKETCH OF THE THEORY

The theory which I have in mind is one which is currently in the process of being developed. The spirit of the approach is shared I believe, by a number of colleagues, although I hasten to add that their emphasis and formalization may well differ from my own in important respects.[4]

The basic idea behind some of the previous work is that structures which were previously derived by means of transformations should in fact be base generated. This point of view was adopted in Brame (1976), although a set of inverse transformations was posited to take over the work of the classical transformations. In Bresnan (1978) the base hypothesis is adopted together with a more interpretively based account of several alternations which were previously treated by transformations, in particular, the passive. Bresnan introduces functional structures as components of lexical specifications in conjunction with operations on functional structures. She assumes that the passive construction is to be treated by a universal operation on functional structure. In Brame (1978a, 1978b), the functional framework is elaborated and refined and pursued in terms of binding structures. In Yildirim (1978) an investigation of causative constructions is undertaken.

In what follows, I would like to take what I consider to be a natural next step. Let us eliminate the phrase structure rules in favor of a still more surface approach. We will then provide a set of rules of composition in accord with the suggestion in Brame (1978a, p. 122, fn. 17). We will then be working directly off the surface strings of lexical items, or more accurately, of phonological words. Within such a theory, it is no longer possible to simply gloss over lexical specifications of the words that play a role in the analysis. Rather, lexical specifications must be provided to ensure the proper functioning of the grammar as a whole.

In this spirit, partial lexical specifications corresponding to *John, man, you, the, met,* and *left* are provided below.

(38) John; $A^{n[x]}$

(39)   man; $A^{nom[s]}$

(40)   the; F^{det}, __$(A^{nom[x]})$

(41)   met; F^v, __$(A^{n[o]})$

(42)   left; F^v, __ or __$(A^{n[o]})$

Instead of phrase structure rules, we define the composition function $\mathcal{F}$.
A tentative and fragmentary formulation is provided below.

(43)   a.   For each phonological word a, compose a as some grammatical
              function A^x or F^y.

        b.   Compose F^v or $\overparen{F^v\ A^x}$ as F^{vp}

        c.   Compose $\overparen{F^d\ A^x}$ as $A^{n[x]}$.

        d.   Compose $\overparen{A^x\ F^{vp}}$ as A^s.

In (43a), the x and y range over appropriate values for arguments and
functions. For example, arguments include nominal singular arguments
such as *man* in (39), np arguments such as *John* in (38), etc. Functions
include verbal functions such as *met* (which is really complex in this case)
in (41), preposition functions such as *into* which is $F^{p[dir]}$, etc. It is quite
conceivable that some of the rules in (43) can be generalized. For example, (43b) and (43c) are similar in that they compose head functions with
their arguments.

    We now ask whether the following example is a well-formed sentence
of English. Since it obviously is, we must illustrate the means by which a
syntactic interpretation is built up.

(44)   The man met you.

Applying rule (43a) to the string of phonological words, one possible
result is the following.

(45) F^{det} $A^{nom[s]}$ F^v $A^{n[x]}$
          | | | |
       the   man   met   you

Applying rules (43b) and (43c) to (45), we obtain the following.

(46)

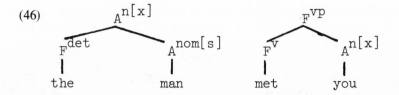

Finally, applying rule (43d) to (46), we obtain the following.

(47)

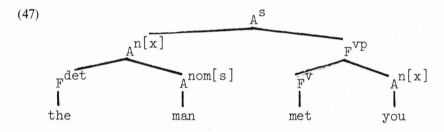

Further rules will specify the x of the two instances of $A^{n[x]}$ as s or o, depending on whether the function is subject or object.

We now wish to check the result for well-formedness. This involves an indexing procedure in conjunction with a convention for establishing equivalences.

(48) a. Let T be a term dominating a lexical category a. If $(a; T, ...) \in$ Lexicon, then assign T a distinct index i, which we may write as T: i.

b. Let T be a term directly dominating terms $T_1 ... T_n$ and let T_1 be indexed by i. Then set T equivalent to the functional structure of the lexical item indexed by i and substitute the indices of $T_1, T_2, ..., T_n$ for corresponding terms.

Applying (48a) to our example, we obtain the following result.

(49)

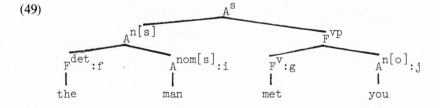

We now apply (48b) to (49). The lexical item *the* corresponds to the lexical entry $\langle$the; F^{det}, __$(A^{nom[x]})\rangle$. The complete functional structure is the function F^{det} taken with its argument $A^{nom[x]}$, which is $F^{det}(A^{nom[x]})$. Hence we set $A^{n[s]}$ equivalent to $F^{det}(A^{nom[s]})$ and substitute corresponding indices to get $f(i)$, which can be indicated as k, the index of $A^{n[s]}$. A similar procedure applies to the F^{vp} function and we obtain the following partial interpretation.

(50)

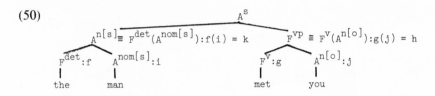

By a similar procedure, we set A^s equivalent to $F^{vp}(A^{n[s]})$ and substitute corresponding indices to yield the complete interpretation $h(k)$, which can be represented as the propositional index p.

With this fragmentary grammar, we succeed in providing a functional interpretation for the simple example provided in (44). By contrast, an example such as (51) cannot be provided a complete interpretation.

(51) *The man met.

Incompleteness follows from the fact that *met* rquires an object as indicated in its lexical specification in (51).[5] When we attempt to interpret (51), we obtain the following partial interpretation.

(52)

$$A^s \equiv F^{vp}(A^{n[s]}) \equiv (F^V(A^{n[o]}))(A^{n[s]}): \boxed{(g(A^{n[o]})(k)}$$

$$A^{n[s]} \equiv F^{det}(A^{nom[s]}):f(i) = k \qquad F^{vp} \equiv F^V(A^{n[o]}):g(A^{n[o]})$$

$$F^{det}:f \qquad A^{nom[s]}:i \qquad F^V:g$$

the   man   met

The absence of the required object is evident when we look at the final interpretation structure $(g(A^{n[o]}))(k)$, which has been boxed in (52).

To account for the deviance of such examples, the initial part of the following principle was proposed in Brame (1978a).[6]

(53) Incompleteness

A string $a_1 \ldots a_n$ is incompletely interpreted with respect to an interpretation φ provided there is a term T in φ corresponding to no index or provided there is no index in φ corresponding to a_i for some i, where $1 \leqslant i \leqslant n$.

In the earlier work, the filtering device was termed the *Principle of Functional Deviance*. The second part of (53) will account for the deviance of cases such as *John slept the mouse* and a full range of examples, as we shall see below in section 4.

3. TENTATIVE SOLUTIONS

Partial solutions to the problems mentioned in section 1 can be provided within the proposed framework provided we extend the theory in natural ways. Let us turn first to the question of binding.

3.1 *Binding*

Consider once again the deviant example given in (51). The deviance can be ameliorated if we append additional words to get the following.

(54)   the girl who(m) the man met

Let us consider the embedded sentential structure *who the man met*. Although there is no phonological word following *met* which could function as the object required by its lexical specification, intuitively we wish to interpret *who* as the object in this case. In fact, this can be done without making the traditional assumption of transformationalists, i.e. without assuming that (54) derives from a more abstract source with post-verbal object. The relative clause of (54) can be interpreted directly provided we posit an appropriate lexical specification for the relative pronoun *who* in conjunction with a general operation on functional structure. A partial lexical specification is provided below in (55).

(55)   who; $A^{n[x]}$, $(F^{rel}$ (__)) (A^s)

Although *who* is taken to be an unspecified np argument, it has the ultimate character of an operator, for it is composed to yield the relative operator F^{rel} ($A^{n[x]}$) taken with its argument A^s. After the interpretive procedures apply, we obtain the following partial interpretation.

(56)

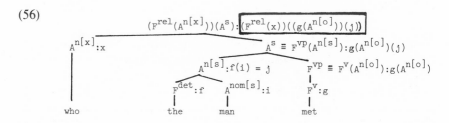

Here we obtain the partial interpretation indicated in the box to the right of the colon in the top line of (56). It is to this functional structure that the general rule of binding proposed in Brame (1978a) applies. This rule is repeated below as (57).

(57)   Operator Binding [OB]:

Let $F(a)$ be an operator with index a and let (... T ...) be its scope, where T is a term in the accessible scope of $F(a)$ and of the same type as that indexed by a. Then identify T with a and index F.

The result of applying OB to the partial interpretation of (56) is illustrated below in (58).

(58) $(F^{rel}\ (x))\ ((g(A^{n[o]}))\ (j)$

$(h(x))\ ((g(x))\ (j))$

Since (56) is now completely interpreted, the principle of incompleteness will be inapplicable. The relative clause itself can be taken as an argument $A^{s[rel]}$ and provided a single index p. It itself must then be composed with its head *the girl* in (54), by a rule of anaphora.

Operator Binding is a general rule. It is not formulated so as to apply only to relative clauses. Other operators will be provided an interpretation utilizing OB and such operators include the question operator $F^q(a)$, the topic operator $F^{top}(a)$, the focus operator $F^{foc}(a)$, and the comparative operators $F^{c[x]}(x)$. There are perhaps others as well, such as the exclamatory operator $F^{ex}(a)$ and the contrastive operator $F^{con}(a)$. If heads of syntactic constructions can be interpreted as any of these operators under appropriate conditions, then OB will apply to bind the appropriate arguments. This is done without any necessity for the usual assumption (of transformational grammar) that there is an NP category following the verb in relative clauses such as (54). The object argument is interpreted in terms of the lexical specification of the verb *met* in this case.

Not only does OB generalize across operator types, it also generalizes across category types. Thus, if the operator suffix happens to be a prepositional phrase argument or a sentential argument, OB will apply nonetheless. This analysis succeeds to some extent, then, in satisfying criteria (i) and (ii) of the binding problem elaborated in subsection 1.1. Points (iii) and (iv) are also covered by this analysis. To see this, let us return to the deviant examples provided in (2)–(6) above.

These examples violate the accessible scope condition associated with OB. Accessible scope is defined as follows:

Def.   Let $O(a)$ be an operator with index a and let (... T ...) be its scope (i.e. its argument structure), where T is a term. If $P(b)$ is an operator falling in the scope of $O(a)$, we say that the *accessible scope* of $O(a)$ includes all material falling in the scope of $O(a)$ which does not fall in the scope of $P(b)$ for all $P(b)$.

The effect of incorporating accessible scope into OB is that of prohibiting certain functional terms from being identified with indices of operator suffixes. This in turn gives rise to incomplete interpretation by the principle of incompleteness noted above.

Note also that the filtering property displayed in terms of (8) is also accounted for. In the case of such examples, there is no term which could be identified with the operator suffix. Consequently the binding rule will not apply, from which it follows that the operator prefix in each case will not be indexed. Hence, again, the principle of incompleteness will apply and such examples will be declared deviant.

Above it was noted that OB generalizes across categories. However, it is necessary that the associated lexical representations of the operator words reflect the operator structure before an interpretation can be built up which will give rise to binding. Some *wh*-words, for example, function as determiners and require the presence of their argument structure. Such examples include the following questions.

(59)   a. Whose books did Mary read?
        b. Which clepsydra did Bill use?
        c. How many eggs can you eat?

A *wh*-word such as *whose* will have to be given a partial lexical specification such as (60)

(60)   whose; F^{pos}, $F^q(\_\_(A^{nom[x]}))$ $(A^{s[q]})$

Now the presence of $A^{nom[x]}$ in the functional structure of *wh*-determiners such as *whose, which,* and *how many* will ensure that the following examples are not completely interpreted.

(61)   a. *Whose did Mary read books?
       b. *Which did Bill use clepsydra?
       c. *How many can you eat eggs?

To be sure, *whose, which,* and *how many* also function as np arguments, thus providing for examples such as the following.

(62)   a. Whose did Mary read?
       b. Which did Bill use?
       c. How many can you eat?

But this simply entails an elaboration of the lexical specifications of these words to include the additional argument structure. For example, *whose* must include in addition to the structure in (60), a representation as $A^{n[x]}$. In neither case, however, will the examples in (61) receive a complete interpretation. In the latter case where *whose* is interpreted as $A^{n[x]}$ we will be left with an example characterized by the filtering property reminiscent of (8). In this case, we will be left with an uninterpreted operator prefix. In the former case, where *whose* is interpreted as F^{pos}, we will be left with an uninterpreted argument $A^{nom[x]}$. Hence both types of examples are incompletely interpreted. Consequently examples such as those provided in (61) are deviant.

This result follows without ad hoc theoretical elaboration. There is no need for special constraints such as the Left Branch Condition proposed in Ross (1967) or the Relativized A/A proposed in Bresnan (1976). Rather, the lexicon in conjunction with general interpretive procedures plays a central role. There is some hope that the vast array of constraints and conditions of transformational grammar can be dispensed with.

A key to the realization that long-distance transformations should be eliminated in favor of more general nontransformational analyses is that questions, relative clauses, focus constructions, and others do not really involve structural distortions which cannot be treated on the surface. A first attempt at generalizing the full range of constructions can be found in Brame (1976), where a general rule of COMP-Insertion was proposed together with base generated questions, relative clauses, and comparative clauses, with syntactic heads in situ. The generalized filtering problem was accounted for by incorporating an inverse cyclic checking procedure. Thus, although an example such as *the boy who(m) Mary saw Bill* could be base generated within the proposed framework, after COMP-Insertion, a violation of subcategorization resulted, viz. *the boy [Mary saw who(m) Bill]* or *the boy [Mary saw Bill who(m)]*, etc. Although this analysis is deficient in various ways, I think it can be seen as a step in the right direction. In particular, there is an obvious similarity here between the subcategorization violation and incompleteness within the framework advocated above.

A second proposal for treating the examples cited in subsection 1.1 can be found in Chomsky (1977). Although this analysis includes much interesting discussion, in my opinion it is in some respects a step backwards from the earlier proposal incorporating base generated structures. The analysis clings to tradition and provides for underlying relative clauses, questions, etc. as "complete sentences". It incorporates an inverse variant of my earlier rule of COMP-Insertion, now called "Move *wh*-phrase". This analysis clearly misses an important generalization since a second "interpretive" rule is required to introduce variables in the position of traces left behind by the movement rule, cf. Chomsky (1977, rule (38)). The analysis also involves a number of theoretical elaborations, including traces, special constraints such as SSC, PIC, RAOAC, special housekeeping rules, and many many other assumptions, cf. Brame (1978a, 1978b). Later developments include a proliferation of filters, cf. below and Brame (1979).

A third analysis is that detailed in Brame (1978a, 1978b) in which base generated structures are again provided together with the general treatment outlined above. The analysis provided here differs only insofar as base rules are eliminated in favor of rules of composition.

To my knowledge, there are no convincing arguments against the "direct" approach to long-distance structures as opposed to the traditional approach involving movement rules. In Chomsky (1977), there is a comment in footnote 16 to the effect that a direct treatment is not "a meaningful alternative to the transformational analysis as a movement rule, for reasons discussed in Chomsky (1975c)." When we consult this reference, however, we find no argument against the direct treatment. By contrast, Wasow (1977) attempts to provide arguments against a direct approach to questions and relative clauses by appealing to well-known facts about contraction. A detailed discussion of these arguments is provided in my forthcoming book *Linguistic Problems* in which an analysis of contracted elements is provided. Within the framework of this analysis contractions are contractions and Wasow's facts are handled in a straightforward way. It turns out that examples such as *Where does John think the party's,* *John has eaten more beans than Bill's*, etc. cannot be provided a complete interpretation.

Although I think there are no real arguments against a direct approach to questions, relative clauses, and other binding constructions, it does appear that there are arguments against the traditional indirect approach, including its modern variant proposed in Chomsky (1977).

The most obvious argument against the indirect approach within the framework of Chomsky (1977) has already been mentioned, namely, it misses an important generalization. Both a movement rule is proposed to move *wh*-phrases into COMP position and an interpretive rule is needed to identify the deposited trace with the index of the COMP phrase. Certainly this duplication is to be avoided. The obvious move is to eliminate the movement into COMP altogether and to state matters once and for all, as is done above in terms of Operator Binding.

A second argument against the indirect transformational approach is noted, interestingly, in Chomsky and Lasnik (1977), where examples such as the following are drawn from Bresnan (1977).

(63)   a man *who* Mary called __ an idiot and June called __ a cretin

Chomsky and Lasnik remark: "A question arises, then, as to how the *wh*-phrase can be moved simultaneously from the two positions marked by __ [in this example] to the single italicized position ...; no existing theory permits anything of the sort" (pp. 490–1). Indeed, this is so, indicating that theories incorporating movement from the positions marked __ to the italicized position approach the question in the wrong way. It should be noted that the analysis advanced above in terms of Operator Binding can account for (63) without further ad hoc elaboration. The rule of OB does allow binding into conjoined sentences when the arguments are of the same type! By contrast, Chomsky and Lasnik must make an additional assumption: "... the *wh*-word appears [to derive] from the first clause while some sort of deletion applies in the second" (p. 491). This new assumption involving "some sort of deletion" is a consequence of assuming a movement analysis as opposed to a direct interpretive approach.

Now if the *wh*-phrases really derive from a more abstract sentence internal position, as in transformational grammar, we might expect them to exhibit a distribution sentence-internally identical to that of the *wh*-phrases in head-position. The distribution does not quite coincide, however, as noted in Brame (1978a).

(64)   a.   What the hell did you see?
        b.   *You saw what the hell?
        c.   *You saw something the hell.
(65)   a.   Who the hell is he talking about?
        b.   *He is talking about who the hell.
        c.   *He is talking about someone the hell.

Before turning to the next topic, let us consider for a moment examples of the following type, involving scopal predicates.

(66)   a.   Sonatas are easy to play on this violin.
        b.   This violin is easy to play sonatas on.
        c.   It is easy to play sonatas on this violin.

It is well-known that a traditional assumption is that such examples are related transformationally. By contrast, in Brame (1976), examples such as (66a) and (66b) are not derived from (66c). Rather, (66a) and (66b) were base generated. This analysis is a more radical departure from tradition than the analysis mentioned in Ross (1967) and subsequently adopted in Lasnik and Fiengo (1974) which incorporates structures such as *this violin is easy to play sonatas on it* corresponding to the underlying representation for (66b), for example.

Now it is interesting that examples such as (66a) and (66b) illustrate the filtering property. Thus, the following examples must be ruled out.

(67)   a. *Sonatas are easy to play tunes on this violin.
        b. *This violin is easy to play sonatas on this cello.

An account of this property is provided in Brame (1976). However, the fact that such examples exhibit the filtering property should perhaps clue us to the possibility that such examples involve binding. If so, then we should expect to find the accessible scope property as well. This we do find, as illustrated below.

(68) *question-scopal predicate*
a. *Which sonatas is this violin easy to play __ on __?
rel-scopal predicate
b. *the sonatas which this violin is easy to play __ on __
top-scopal predicate
c. *These sonatas this violin is easy to play __ on __.
foc-scopal predicate
d. *It is this sonata that this violin is easy to play __ on __.

Such examples illustrate the prohibition against operating into scopal predication contexts by questioning, relativizing, topicalizing, and focussing. It is also not permitted to scopally predicate into question contexts, relative clause contexts, etc.

(69) *scopal predicate-question*
a. *This violin would be easy to ask Mary which sonatas she plays __ on __.
cf. It would be easy to ask Mary which sonatas she plays on this violin.

scopal predicate-rel
b. *These sonatas are easy to tune the violin that Mary plays __ on __.
cf. It is easy to tune the violin that Mary plays these sonatas on.

Similarly, it is not possible to scopally predicate into a scopal predication context.

(70) *scopal predicate-scopal predicate*
*This violin would be hard for these sonatas to be easy for Mary to play __ on __.
cf. It would be hard for these sonatas to be easy for Mary to play on this violin.

There are, then, excellent grounds for concluding that we are dealing with another instance of binding. One of the virtues of the analysis proposed by Chomsky in his *wh*-movement paper is that there is an attempt at generalizing the scopal predication cases with the others. However, as reiterated here, these processes do not involve movement. Nor do the scopal predication cases involve *wh*-phrases.

Within the theory offered here, it would not be implausible to treat the formative *to* as a kind of operator, perhaps as an operator prefix of a scopal predicate operator F^{sp} ($A^{n[x]}$), as indicated below in terms of a partial lexical specification for *to*.

(71) to; F^{sp}, $(\_(A^{n[x]}))$ (A^{vp})

(Of course *to* will be provided with additional functional structure.) We would then interpret an example such as *John is easy to please* as something approximating (72).

(72) $f(g((F^{sp}$ $(A^{n[x]}))$ $(h(A^{n[o]})))$ (i)

where *John* : i, *is* : f, g : *easy*, and h : *please*

The operator prefix F^{sp} is indexed and a rule is required to identify the subject index i with the operator suffix $A^{n[x]}$. Finally, OB will then be applicable and will bind $A^{n[o]}$ as i.

Such an analysis would involve no special *wh*-phrase nor a special deletion rule as proposed in Chomsky (1977).

3.2 *VP-Ellipsis*

Let us now turn to the problem enunciated in subsection 1.2, termed the Multiple Ambiguity Problem. In particular, let us first consider the lack of 4-way ambiguity of the following example.

(73) These are flying planes and those are too.

To treat such examples it is necessary to introduce a partial lexical specification for conjunctions such as *and*.

(74) and; $F^{con[\&]}$, $\_(X_1, X_2, ..., X_n)$

It is intended that a lexical item such as *and* is interpreted as a kind of function which selects any number of arguments of type X.

It is also necessary to provide an analysis of the auxiliary system of English. Within the framework advocated here, there are no transformations. In particular, there is no affix-hopping transformation as in the standard theory, cf. Chomsky (1957). Rather, we must provide for the relevant auxiliary phrases directly, making more use of the lexicon, as in Brame (1978c).

To see how this might be accomplished, let us take the phrase *flying planes* in the verbal sense. A representation for the verb *fly* might be something like (75).

(75) fly; F^v, __$(A^{n[o]})$

Of course it is necessary to provide for additional functional structure to account for the intransitive use of *fly*, etc.

Now we would like to say that *flying*, like *fly*, can select a direct object argument. Suppose we enter the suffix *ing* in the lexicon as a kind of function, the progressive function.

(76) ing; F^{prog}, __(F^v)

Now the fact that *flying* selects the identical argument structure as *fly* can be expressed by the following redundancy rule which operates on lexical specifications to yield new lexical entries.

(77) Aux Redundancy:

If (a; F^x, __(F^v)) and (b; F^v, ...) ϵ Lexicon, form a new lexical entry L = (ba; F^x (F^v), ...).

Applying the redundancy rule (77) to (75) and (76), we obtain the new lexical entry *flying*, indicated below.

(78) flying; F^{prog} (F^v), __$(A^{n[o]})$

We might even provide the composition function F^{prog} (F^v) with a coarser specification such as $F^{prog\text{-}part}$ and call it the progressive participle function. More importantly, we may consider *flying planes* as a special kind of argument, a progressive participle argument, represented as $A^{v[prog]}$. We could then provide the auxiliary verb *be* with the following lexical representation.

(79) be; F^v, __$(A^{v[prog]})$

In addition to the lexical specifications provided, it is necessary to extend the rules of composition to include the following.

(80) a. Compose $\overset{\frown}{X_1}\,\overset{\frown}{X_2}\,...\,\overset{\frown}{X_{n-1}}\,\overset{\frown}{F^{con[\&]}}\,X_n$ as $F^{con[\&]}\,(X_1, X_2, ..., X_{n-1}, X_n)$

  b. Compose $F^{prog}\,\overset{\frown}{(F^v)}\,A^x$ as $(F^{prog}(F^v))(A^x)$

With these lexical specifications, composition rules, and indexing procedures, we may now derive an interpretation for the left conjunct of example (73). Rather than provide the complete tree, the terminal interpretation structure will be provided.

(81) $(F^v(A^{v[prog]}))\,(A^{n[s]})$: $(f(i))\,(j)$

  where $f = are$, $i = flying\ planes$, $j = these$

Notice that i indexes *flying planes* in the progressive participial sense, not the np sense of a subject complement. To derive the other interpretation, we must extend the lexical specification of the verb *be* to permit subject complement arguments.

(82) be; F^v, $\underline{\quad}(A^{v[prog]})$ or $\underline{\quad}(A^{n[sc]})$ or $\underline{\quad}(A^{a[sc]})$

Noun phrases interpreted as $A^{n[x]}$ will qualify as subject complements and adjectives which are interpreted as $A^{a[sc]}$ in their predicative function (vs. their attributive function in which they are F^a) also qualify as arguments of *be*. The second reading for the left conjunct of example (73) is then the following.

(83) $(F^v(A^{n[sc]}))(A^{n[s]})$: $(f(i))(j)$

  where $f = are$, $i = flying\ planes$, $j = these$

Under this interpretation, *flying planes* is a subject complement, not a progressive participial phrase.

Consider now the right conjunct of (73), repeated below as (84).

(84) Those are too.

We may derive two partial interpretations for (84).

(85)   a. $(F^v(A^{v[prog]}))(A^{n[s]}) : (f(A^{v[prog]}))(j)$
        where $f = are, j = those$

       b. $(F^v(A^{n[sc]}))(A^{n[s]}) : (f(A^{n[sc]}))(j)$
        where $f = are, j = those$

If there is no context, (84) will be declared deviant under either of the two interpretations of (85). Clearly, we require an operation on functional structure to identify the unindexed term $A^{v[prog]}$ in the partial interpretation of the right conjunct with the index i of (81) and to identify the unindexed term $A^{n[sc]}$ of (85b) with the index i in (83). To see this more clearly, let us collect together the two conjuncts as they would be interpreted. There are in fact four possibilities.

(86)   a. $F^{con[\&]}(F_1^v (A_1^{v[prog]}))(A_1^{n[s]}), (F_2^v(A_2^{v[prog]}))(A_2^{n[s]}))$:
        $h((f(i))(j), (g(A_2^{v[prog]}))(k))$

        where $h = and, f = are, i = flying\ planes$, etc.

       b. $F^{con[\&]}((F_1^v(A_1^{n[sc]}))(A_1^{n[s]}), (F_2^v(A_2^{n[sc]}))(A_2^{n[s]}))$:
        $h((f(i))(j), (g(A_2^{n[sc]}))(k))$

        where $h = and, f = are, i = flying\ planes$, etc.

       c. $F^{con[\&]}((F_1^v(A^{v[prog]}))(A_1^{n[s]}), (F_2^v(A^{n[sc]}))(A_2^{n[s]}))$:
        $h((f(i))(j), (g(A^{n[sc]}))(k))$

       d. $F^{con[\&]}((F_1^v(A^{n[sc]}))(A_1^{n[s]}), (F_2^v(A^{v[prog]}))(A_2^{n[s]}))$
        $h((f(i))(j), (g(A^{v[prog]}))(k))$

Now in order to ensure the necessary identification between the unspecified arguments in (86a) and (86b), the following operation on functional structure can be adopted.

(87)   Ellipsis:

       Let i and A^x be included in a partial interpretation φ such that i indexes an argument of the same type as A^x for some x. Then identify A^x with i.

By employing this rule of Ellipsis, we succeed in deriving a complete interpretation for (86a) and (86b), but we fail to derive a complete interpretation in the case of (86c) and (86d) since the index i in (86c) does index an argument of the same type as $A^{n[sc]}$ and the index i does not index an argument of type $A^{v[prog]}$ in (86d). It follows, then, that the related example (83) is 2-ways ambiguous, not 4-ways ambiguous. This constitutes a solution to MAP discussed in subsection 1.2 and can be extended to examples (23a-d).

The theory developed here seems to be suitable for handling the discourse examples as well, cf. (25). Coarser discourse relations are certainly compatible provided we append suitable rules of discourse composition. Some initial work with discourse relations was attempted in Brame (1978b).

This analysis should also extend to examples such as the following.

(88) a. John has eaten more beans than Mary has.
      b. Sally will learn less than Mary will.
      c. His mind is not as quick as yours is.
      d. Sue is running faster than Ed is.

Some details have not been discussed. For example, it is necessary to provide a lexical representation for *too* and an appropriate rule of composition to ensure that a complete interpretation is provided for example (83). We might take *too* and its negative counterpart *either* to be functions and provide lexical specifications to reflect this characterization. A number of questions arise in the course of attempting such an analysis. For example, there are apparently a number of restrictions on the distribution of *too* and *either* as the following examples illuminate.

(89) a. John has eaten or Bill has too.
      b. John eats less than Bill does too.
      c. John has eaten or Bill hasn't either.
      d. John eats less than Bill doesn't either.

The functions *too* and *either* seem to involve a kind of parallelism which when absent leads to deviance. In (89), it appears that *or* and *than* imply nonparallelism of the requisite type. Whether or not we should make parallelism a necessary condition for indexing of *too* and *either* is a question which must ultimately be confronted.

3.3 *Pronominalization and Ellipsis as Anaphora*

As noted in subsection 1.3, the pronominalization facts and the ellipsis facts point to a deeper generalization and pose somewhat of a dilemma for the standard theory of transformational grammar. Both Lakoff (1976) and Bresnan (1978) have recognized this fact.

> What is unexplained in the transformational theory is why verb phrase ellipsis is subject to the same conditions as pronominalization ... [Bresnan (1978, p. 47)]

Bresnan points to what appears to be a promising solution. She proposes that Lasnik's Noncoreferentiality Rule be formulated in terms of indexing, presumably generalized to accommodate the ellipsis facts in addition to the pronoun cases. (Cf. Lasnik (1976), Reinhart (1976) and DeCarrico (1978) on noncoreferentiality.) Lasnik's rule is repeated below.

(90)   Noncoreferentiality Rule:

   If NP_1 precedes and commands NP_2 and NP_2 is not a pronoun, then NP_1 and NP_2 are disjoint in reference.

The analysis developed in the preceding subsection is in the spirit of Bresnan's suggestion. This suggests that we attempt to extend the ellipsis rule (87) to include pronouns and the relevant precede and command relations.

(91)   Let i and $A^{y[x]}$ be included in a partial interpretation φ. Then index $A^{y[x]}$ as i provided the following conditions hold:
   (i) i indexes $A^{y[z]}$ for some z
   (ii) $A^{y[x]}$ does not precede and command $A^{y[z]}$ in the tree associated with φ

This rule allows us to index an uninterpreted pronoun or verb phrase argument with i provided the argument indexed by i and the pronoun or verb phrase argument are of the same general type $A^{n[x]}$ or $A^{v[x]}$. It furthermore prohibits indexing when the uninterpreted argument precedes and commands the argument indexed by i. Rule (91), which we may call Anaphora, should also generalize to nominal arguments of functions such as *some, any, many*, etc.

   Now if it is correct to generalize the latter phenomena with ellipsis, we might expect to find an analogue of the multiple ambiguity problem in these domains. In fact we do encounter MAP here as well. This is illustrated in the following examples.

(92)   a. I saw some boy[z] flying planes and Bill saw some too.
   b. Bill has many pipes which you must look up and you have many too.

The ambiguity of such examples can be illuminated in terms of the following.

(93) a. I saw some boys flying planes.
      b. I saw some boys' flying planes.
(94) a. Bill has many pipes up which you must look.
      b. Bill has many pipes which you must look up in the catalogue.

Again, as with the earlier examples of 1.2, we see that there is no 4-way ambiguity in (92), only 2-way ambiguity. It appears, then, that we are indeed dealing with a more far-reaching process of anaphora which cuts across argument structure.

3.4 *Binding and Anaphora*

Turning back to the problem of the interaction of binding and ellipsis, let us consider the following discourse.

(95) a. John is eating.
      b. Who is?

There is no difficulty in interpreting this discourse. The relative pronoun *who* stands for the subject and does not therefore interact with the anaphor of (95b). On the other hand, the following example does exhibit such interaction.

(96) a. John is eating.
      b. *What is he?

The partial interpretation associated with (96b) is provided below.

(97) $F^q(A^{n[x]})((F^v(A^{v[prog]})(A^{n[s]})) : F^q(x)((f(A^{v[prog]})(i))$
      where $x = what, f = is, i = he = John$

In (97) it is assumed that a prior application of Anaphora has identified *he* with *John*. This identification is not of concern. Now, if we apply Anaphora to (97), we can in fact identify $A^{v[prog]}$ with the index of *eating beans* in the interpretation associated with (96a). This identification, however, has the consequence that Operator Binding will be inapplicable to (97). Hence the operator prefix F^q will not be indexed, with the net result that (96b) will not be fully interpreted. Hence by the principle of incompleteness, this example is ruled out. On the other hand, we can also operate on a finer representation of the partial interpretation associated with (96b). For example, the following is equivalent in the intended sense to (97).

(98) $F^q(A^{n[x]})((F^v(F^{prog\text{-}part}(A^{n[o]}))(A^{n[s]})) : F^q(x)((f(F^{prog\text{-}part}(A^{n[o]}))(i))$

     where $x = what, f = is, i = he$

To this partial interpretation OB is now applicable, yielding the following partial interpretation.

(99) $g(x)((f(F^{prog\text{-}part}(x))(i))$

But now Anaphora is inapplicable since the coarser argument $A^{v[prog]}$ is no longer a completely uninterpreted argument. Hence there is again no way of providing a complete interpretation for (96b). In consequence, this example is deviant. Or to put it differently, it simply cannot be interpreted.

Now if binding is correctly expressed as a general process like OB, then we expect to encounter similar interaction results and we do.

(100)   *Root Q*
       a. *What did he?
          cf. What did he eat?

       Embedded Q
       b. *I asked what John had eaten but not what Bill had.
          cf. I asked what John had eaten but not what Bill had eaten.
             I knew that John had eaten but not that Bill had.

       Relative Clause
       c. *I saw the boy who Harry is arguing with and who Sam is.
          cf. I saw the boy who Harry is arguing with and who Sam is
             arguing with.

       Topicalization
       d. *This boy John might nominate and that boy Bill might.

Pseudo-Cleft
e. *What John is eating and what Harry is may not be fit for you.
    cf. What John is eating and what Harry is eating may not be fit
    for you.

Focus
f. *It was salt that Harry objected to and pepper that Mary did.
    cf. It was salt that Harry objected to and pepper that Mary ob-
    jected to.

Root Exclamation
g. *What big teeth you have and what big eyes you do!
    cf. What big teeth you have and what big eyes you have!

Embedded Exclamation
h. *I'm surprised at what big teeth you have and at what big eyes
    John does!
    cf. I'm surprised at what big teeth you have and at what big
    eyes John has.

Free Relative
i. *I'll buy what you are selling and what Bill is.
    cf. I'll buy what you are selling and what Bill is selling.

Appositive Relative
j. *John, who Mary likes but who Bill doesn't, is my friend.
    cf. John, who Mary likes but who Bill doesn't like, is my
    friend.

In (100) I have attempted to give clear-cut examples of the deviance that
results when interaction is attempted. Some of these examples can perhaps be made to appear better if the mind is misdirected with additional
adverbial and scopal-like elements. My feeling is that the examples should
be judged deviant. If so, then, again, the parallelism suggests that it is
correct to treat binding in a general way as suggested in 3.1.

Several examples of interaction have been noted in Sag (1976) and
Williams (1977), where explanations are attempted. Williams' analysis has
more in common with that proposed here than Sag's.

Now the theory advanced here makes an interesting prediction. To see
this consider the following examples.

(101) a. I wanted to see John and I did see John.
       b. I wanted to see John and I did.
(102) a. I wanted to see John and did see John.
       b. I wanted to see John and did.

The examples listed in (102) involve conjoined verb phrases and are not derived from more abstract underlying structures.

The following contrast is predicted in accord with the explanation provided above.[7]

(103)   a.   John, who I wanted to see and who I did see, is my friend.
        b.   *John, who I wanted to see and who I did, is my friend.

But a further prediction follows. The appositive relative related to (102b), as opposed to (101), should be fully grammatical.

(104)   John, who I wanted to see and did, is my friend.

The operator *who* is the head of the sentence *I wanted to see and did.* Since this sentence involves a conjoined verb phrase, not a conjoined sentence, there is no operator associated with the right conjunct per se. Hence, after the index of *who* has been associated with the object argument $A^{n[o]}$ of *see*, Anaphora can proceed to supply an appropriate index for the argument of *did*, corresponding to *see who*. The problem that arises in connection with (103b) simply does not arise here in connection with (104). This difference is predicted by the theory provided here.

There is still a further prediction made by the theory advocated here. Recall, above in subsection 1.1, it was noted that operators tend to generalize across argument types. We now have in hand a new set of argument types, namely, the $A^{v[x]}$ arguments, of which we have had occasion to consider $A^{v[prog]}$. Others include $A^{v[perf]}$, $A^{v[pas]}$, etc., corresponding to *eaten beans, eaten by John,* etc. We might therefore expect to find some *wh*-type operator which subsumes this type of argument as well. And in fact we do, as shown in the following examples.

(105)   a. They say John is eating beans, which he is.
        b. They say John has eaten beans, which he has.
        c. They say John will eat beans, which he will.
        d. They say John eats beans, which he does.

The striking point about these examples is that they are grammatical, even though they appear to exhibit the interaction property. But, in fact, the grammaticality of such examples is predicted by the theory. We let operator words such as *which* be interpreted as $A^{v[x]}$ arguments in addition to $A^{n[x]}$ and let Anaphora identify the pronominal-like argument head with the preceding argument index. It is this index which is then identified with the argument structure of the auxiliaries in (105). In other words, Anaphora does not function to fill in the missing auxiliary arguments in (105); Operator Binding does. This accounts for why the interaction property is not observed in these cases.

In conclusion, it seems that the realistic approach offered here does yield some insight into the interaction problem. It also leads to additional predictions which appear to be borne out by the data.

4. CONCLUSION

4.1 *Apparent Arguments Against Pure Surface Theories*

In 3.1 several putative arguments against a direct surface approach to binding were surveyed. Are there any arguments that can be leveled against the more lexically based theory advocated here? For the most part, trace theorists have simply ignored initial work in purer approaches to syntax which eliminate classical transformations. However, more recently Chomsky is reported to have advanced two arguments against surface grammar during the course of his Kant lectures "Rules and Representations" at Stanford (January 1979). I was present for the Sloan Foundation Workshop following these lectures where I learned of these arguments. Apparently Chomsky argued that (i) the "asymmetry" of idioms and (ii) the cross-over facts discussed by Wasow (1972) argue against pure interpretive theories. In the discussion following my own presentation at which Chomsky was present, this assessment was borne out and my work was given the familiar notational variant treatment. Since there are many differences between realistic grammar and trace theory, it will be pointed out in this closing section how realistic grammar surpasses trace theory in providing a much more adequate representation of natural language.

Discussion of the two apparent counterarguments to realistic grammar must be postponed to such a time when the arguments are laid out in an explicit and comprehensible fashion. As I understand the asymmetry argument, Chomsky has claimed that idioms exhibit an asymmetry with respect to deep structure vs. surface structure: there are idioms which reflect deep structure canonical properties only, but there are no idioms that reflect surface structure canonical properties only. Within the theory developed here, there is no distinction between surface and deep structures. Hence Chomsky's argument must somehow translate to the structure of the lexicon if it is to hold. What are the facts concerning this asymmetry? Is there truly some asymmetry? (Tom Wasow informs me that my examples of binding in (64)–(65) may constitute an outright counter-example to Chomsky's argument.) In the absence of published discussion of examples, it is not possible to assess Chomsky's claim.

It is interesting to turn back to an earlier argument against a specific surface analysis provided in Lakoff (1976). This argument concerns the unity of pronominalization and ellipsis, discussed above in 3.3.

> One might be tempted to conclude that since one anaphoric device, definite pronouns, cannot be derived by a deletion transformation, therefore no anaphoric devices can be derived in that way. That is, one might be tempted to assume that anaphoric devices must be derived in some uniform manner.

Of course this is what is claimed above in 3.3 and is suggested in Bresnan (1978). Lakoff goes on to say

> However, it is not at all clear that this is true, since it can be shown that at least one type of anaphoric device must be transformationally derived ... one realizes that definite pronouns and omitted VPs have deep structures of an entirely different nature. The Bach-Peters case seems to show that definite pronouns cannot be derived from repetitions of the full NPs that they refer to. However, omitted VP's *must* [emphasis by Lakoff] be derived from the full VPs to which they refer. The omitted VP cannot just be represented by a blank or a reference index in deep structure. Although definite pronouns cannot be derived by a transformational rule, missing VPs must be ... The reason for this is fairly obvious. Missing VPs can refer to VPs that are derived by transformation, and are not present in deep structure. For example, consider the following:
>
> [14] If John is *shot by Max*, Harry will be.
> [15] If John is *expected by Sam to be shot by Max*, Harry will be.
> [16] If Shakespeare *translates easily into Japanese*, Marlowe will.
> [17] If John is *likely to leave*, Bill will be.
>
> All of the underlined VPs in the preceding examples are transformationally derived; they do not occur as such in deep structure. Since they are not even constituents in deep structure, there is no way to refer to them on that level of analysis. Thus, there is no way of indicating in deep structure what the missing VP will refer to. So, a solution for missing VP's parallel to the no-full-NP solution for definite pronouns ... is not possible.
> [Lakoff (1976, pp. 332–3)]

The fallacy of Lakoff's argument is not unclear. The alternative to the "fairly obvious" conclusion which Lakoff draws is that the examples listed in his [14]–[17] are not transformationally derived. In fact, such facts argue rather strongly for the nontransformational theory advocated above. (Such an argument has been advanced in Brame (1978c) and in Schachter (1978).) We see that Lakoff's observation turns out to be an argument against transformational grammar.

This argument against transformations is similar to that provided in Brame (1976) where it was noted that once Equi is abandoned, the full range of transformation falls with it. Once VP-Deletion as a transformational rule is abandoned, so also a full range of transformations must be eliminated in favor of surface analysis, where lexical items assume a major role.

4.2 *Nonexistence of Empty Nodes and Traces*

One of the basic drawbacks of trace theory is the fact that it is burdened with an excess of theoretically elaborate devices, such as traces and empty nodes. It should be emphasized that such devices are not adopted within the context of realistic grammar as envisaged here. Thus, the interpretations discussed in the preceding pages rely on the functional structure of lexical items for their internal parts. This is true of lexical functions such as verbs and prepositions as well as determiners and specifiers.

There is one area, however, where an explicit account has not been provided. This concerns the subject of binding constructions such as the following.

(106) a. Who left?
      b. the boy who left
      c. I asked who left.
      d. It was John who left.

Recall that *who* is interpreted ultimately as an operator, for example, as $F^q(A^{n[s]})$ in (106a). But we still require the presence of a subject $A^{n[s]}$ if binding is to apply to a composed sentential argument. We must therefore provide for the subject argument and this can be accomplished by providing a rule which will interpret $A^{n[s]}$ in the appropriate position relative to the interpretation tree.

(107) Subject Interpretation:

$$\phi \ \rightarrow \ A^{n[x]} \ / \ F^{op[y]} \_\_F^{vp}$$

In (107) the symbol $F^{op[y]}$ is designed to cover all operators of the $F(A^{n[x]})$ type, for example, the question operator, relative operator, etc. (We assume $F^{op[y]} \equiv F^y(A)$, where y = q, rel, etc.) Notice that we have inserted a general argument $A^{n[x]}$ by rule (107). This causes no difficulty, for we need rules to identify x of np arguments at any rate, as noted earlier. These rules include the following.

(108)   Let $A^{n[x]}$ be the composition of some phonological string.

    (i)   Set $x = s$ / __F^{vp}

    (ii)   Set $x = o$ / F^v__ or F^v $A^{n[x]}$ __

    (iii)   Set $x = dat$ / F^v __

By rule (108i), the x inserted by rule (109) will be s.

Now, let us see how (106a) is interpreted. First, applying the interpretive rules to *who left*, we derive (109).

(109)
$$F^q(A^{n[x]}) : F^q(x) \qquad F^{vp} : f$$
$$A^{n[x]} : x \qquad\qquad F^v : f$$
$$who \qquad\qquad\qquad left$$

Now rule (107) applies, assuming that $F^{op[y]}$ is equivalent to $F^q(A^{n[x]})$ as indicated above. (In fact $F^{op[y]}$ could be included directly in (109).) This gives (110).

(110)
$$F^q(A^{n[x]}) : F^q(x) \qquad A^{n[x]} \qquad F^{vp} : f$$
$$A^{n[x]} : x \qquad\qquad\qquad\qquad F^v : f$$
$$who \qquad\qquad\qquad\qquad\qquad left$$

Now the composition rules and indexing procedure follow, giving the partial interpretation provided in (111).

(111) $F^q(A^{n[x]})((F^{vp}(A^{n[s]})) : F^q(x)((f(A^{n[s]}))$

Now OB can apply to identify $A^{n[s]}$ with x and to index F^q. Analogous steps are involved in the interpretation of the other examples listed in (106).

Now this analysis can be utilized to solve another puzzle. The following distribution of data will serve as an introduction.

(112) a. *Who did you give a book?
       b. *John would be easy to give a book.
       c. *This boy John gave a book.
       d. *the boy who John gave a book
       e. *It was John that Bill gave a book.
       f. *I asked who John gave a book.
       g. *The boy, who John gave a book, is my friend.

It is interesting to note that the full range of binding constructions exhibit deviance when a dative argument serves as the operator suffix. To account for such examples we must first provide a lexical specification for dative verbs such as *give*.

(113)   give; F^v, __$(A^{n[dat]}, A^{n[o]})$ or __$(A^{n[o]}, A^{p[dir]})$

According to (115), *give* is lexically specified to select a dative argument plus object argument or else an object argument plus directional prepositional phrase argument.

Now all along we have been assuming that binding takes place when the operator suffix is $A^{n[x]}$ and the unspecified argument is $A^{n[o]}$, $A^{n[s]}$, etc., as in (111). We now insist that they be identical as indicated by the stipulation in OB that arguments be of the same type. To identify argument suffixes as a specific type, we append the following case to rule (108).

(114)   Set $x = o$, p[dir], p[loc], p[man], ..., s / $(F^x$ __$)A$

Of importance here is the fact that rule (114) does not permit an identification of x as *dat*. That is, it is not possible to identify the operator argument as $A^{n[dat]}$. It then follows that an index standing for $A^{n[dat]}$ cannot be "quantified" into a binding context. From this it follows that examples such as (112a–g) and all similar examples will not be completely interpreted.

With this analysis, we have an explanation for another anomaly, first brought to my attention by Ivonne Bordelois. It concerns the following contrast.

(115)   a. *Who did John promise to sleep?
        b. Who did John persuade to sleep.

If we lexically specify *promise* to select a dative object plus a vp argument, as opposed to *persuade*, which selects a direct object argument plus a vp argument, among others, then we should expect not to be able to completely interpret (115a). We should also expect the full range of judgments to hold.

(116) a. *John would be easy to promise to sleep.
       b. John would be easy to persuade to sleep.
(117) a. *It was John who Bill promised to sleep.
       b. It was John who Bill persuaded to sleep.

There are other approaches to these problems which must be explored within the framework of realistic grammar. For example, we might consider the possibility of imposing restrictions on composition of complex argument structures with F^v functions. This approach might be justified if the following examples are judged deviant.

(118) a. Which book did you give John?
       b. Which book would be easy to give John?
       c. the book which I gave John
       d. This book I gave John.
       e. It was this book that I gave John.
       f. I asked which book you gave John.
       g. the book, which you gave John, is on the table.

Whatever the case may be with the status of these examples, it appears that the realistic grammar framework provides a ray of hope for expressing the obvious generalization.

4.3 *The Missing Argument Phenomenon*

One of the most interesting of puzzles which has been discussed and debated within the framework of transformational grammar involves the status of the following distinction.

(119) a. Who did John say left?
       b. *Who did John say that left?

Let us refer to the problem of accounting for the deviance of (119b) vs. (119a) the *missing argument problem*. Interesting discussion of this problem together with a summary and criticism of previous work can be found in Bresnan (1977). This problem has given rise to constraints such as the Frozen Subject Constraint, cf. Bresnan (1972), indicating by the name that the problem is that of inhibiting the subject from moving to the comp position. Since we are operating within a framework which involves a direct approach to binding, we must now account for why (119b) is uninterpretable.

A new analysis was provided within the framework developed here and presented at the Sloan Workshop at Stanford, cf. Brame (1979a). This analysis involves an extension of rule (107), the rule of Subject Interpretation.

(120) $\phi \rightarrow A^{y[z]} / F^x\_F^{vp}$

where $x = op[w]$ or v

In other words, we allow the interpretation of a subject $A^{n[s]}$ node, for example, as in the earlier case (106), not only after operator functions and before vp functions, but also after verbal functions before vp functions. Thus, there is no problem interpreting (119a). By contrast, (119b) cannot be provided a subject and therefore will be incompletely interpreted. Of course, one can attempt to interpret *that* as the subject of *left* since *that* is multiply specified. However, under this interpretation, binding will never ensue so that the example will be incompletely interpreted. In short, there is no way to completely interpret (119b).

Now rule (120) has been stated in a very general way. Thus, the inserted element need not be $A^{n[s]}$. It can be A^s, instead. This will allow for the interpretation of examples such as (121).

(121) That John left Bill said was obvious.

However, the following will not be interpretable.

(122) *That John left Bill said that __ was obvious.

It should also be possible to insert prepositional phrase arguments. The following example illustrates this case.

(123) In this garage John said could be found three cases of vintage Martel.

Clearly the prepositional phrase argument *in this garage* must be associated with the post verbal position in (123), i.e. after *said*, as predicted by rule (120).

Example (123) is essentially the same type of example adduced in Bresnan (1977, p. 179–80), repeated below.

(124)   It's in these villages that we all believe can be found the best examples of this cuisine.

When I raised the missing argument problem at the recent Sloan Workshop, Chomsky cited the recent unpublished research of Kayne, indicating that its solution concerns the notion subject. Bresnan's example, however, as I pointed out, shows that it is not the notion subject that is at issue. (In response, Chomsky claimed that *in these villages* in (124) is a subject.) A similar set of deviant examples is observed in (125).

(125)   a. *In this garage John said that could be found three cases of vintage Martel.
        b. *It's in these villages that we all believe that can be found the best examples of this cuisine.   [Bresnan, p. 180]

To summarize this subsection, it seems to me once again that some progress can be made toward resolving outstanding problems if we operate within a realistic framework.

4.4 *Chomsky-Lasnik Filters*

In Chomsky and Lasnik (1977), a number of ad hoc filters are proposed to rule out certain ungrammatical examples, including several involving the missing argument phenomenon discussed above. In fact, all of these filters can be dispensed with since they are simply ad hoc special cases of incompleteness (or functional deviance), cf. Brame (1979).

For example, consider the following example discussed by Chomsky and Lasnik.

(126)   *The man left you is my friend.

To account for this example, they propose the following filter.

(127) *[$_{NP}$ NP tense VP]

Notice that (126) can be generated within the Chomsky/Lasnik framework by virtue of their rule of free comp deletion. Thus, they assume that *who* can be freely deleted, even when there is no subject. By contrast, examples such as (126) simply cannot be interpreted within the framework advocated here. It is possible to interpret *the man left you* and *is my friend*, but it is not possible to compose the two, since vp functions do not select sentences such as *the man left you*, cf. Brame (1979).

4.5 *Nonexistence of Ordering*

Many syntacticians have been beating ordering over the head for a number of years. Almost all such critics, however, replace ordering with other ad hoc principles, for example, by principles which seek to establish a universal ordering or by filters and other ad hoc devices. The first real light to be shed on ordering can be found in Bresnan (1978). Bresnan has shown that the ordering facts of transformational grammar *follow* from realistic grammar. There is no need for special principles which simply replace ordering as in other approaches and which have no other function than to establish "universal" orders.

4.6 *New Frontiers: Realistic Phonology*

The approach I have been discussing paves the way for a more realistic approach to phonology, which I have called *lexical phonology*. In particular, the lexical entries provided in realistic grammar can be elaborated in the following way. Let us take the perfective *ed* affix as an example. We have been assuming that it is entered in the lexicon as (128) and that it combines with verbal functions by a general lexical redundancy rule.

(128)   ed; F^v, __(A$^{v[perf]}$)

However, it now seems feasible to take all phonetic realizations of the perfective morpheme to be part of the lexical specification. Thus, (128) will be replaced with (129).

(129)   *d* or *t* or-*id*; F^v, __ (A$^{v[perf]}$)

Within a theory of lexical phonology, phonological rules are not dispensed with as they are in other approaches. Rather, they are interpreted somewhat differently from the standard theory of generative phonology. They can now be interpreted as instructions for combining morphemes by lexical redundancy rules (or alternatively as filters).

For more discussion of this approach, see Brame (to appear), and Yildirim's work on Turkish phonology within such a framework. A goal to shoot for within this theory is to show that ordering follows naturally, as it does in syntax. Guerssel in forthcoming work will show that his important constraints on phonological rules, the Adjacency-Identity Constraint and the Constraint on Assimilation Rules do indeed follow from more general considerations of a theory of lexical phonology. He also shows that the phenomena are far more general than presented in his earlier work, cf. Guerssel (1977, 1978).

4.7 *Linguistic Problems*

The thesis which I insist on emphasizing is this: linguists should be investigating the significant problems that have been discovered over the past two decades of work within the framework of transformational grammar. In Brame (1979a), twenty three such problems are posed and discussed. Several of these problems have been presented here along with tentative solutions. As far as these problems are concerned, a number of outstanding questions remain. Nevertheless, it seems to me that a direct lexically based approach to such problems can provide some illumination and further direction toward an understanding of how they are to be resolved.

NOTES

[1] The distinction between topic operators and contrastive operators is being overlooked for the purposes of this discussion, cf. Brame (1978b, fn. 3).

[2] Of course there is an independent reason for the deviance of (10b) which relates to the prohibition against sentential complements in embedded structures, cf. *Bill believes that that Mary left surprised Harry.*

[3] There is a very interesting fact which will not be explored here. This is the fact that examples (27a), (27b), (30a), and (30b) are in fact well-formed given appropriate pauses and intonation which serve to destroy the natural sequencing of the phrase. Thus, the following are fine.

(i)   I saw *him*—after Mary pointed *Bill* out to me.
(ii)   John thought *she* was tall—when he saw *Mary*

(iii)   John has—if Bill has tasted the beans.

(iv)   Sally can't—if Bill can't leave.

The fact that both the pronouns and auxiliaries function in this way is further evidence that we are dealing with a unified phenomenon. It also seems to be true that the sequencing of a discourse can be broken so that the appropriate relations can be established in the discourse examples in (34) and (35). For example, the following would be fine.

(v)   a. John saw *him*.

     b. Oh yeah? Well I saw *Bill* too.

(vi)   a. John has.

     b. Oh yeah? Well, I've eaten beans too.

The proper treatment of these facts may well have a bearing on the whole question of the proper generalization of ellipsis and pronominalization as anaphora.

[4] Relevant studies include Bresnan (1978), Yildirim (1978), and Brame (1978a, 1978b). For an analysis of binding very much in the spirit of my own, see Woolford (to appear).

[5] In general all lexical specifications provided here are partial. Relevant lexical structure is omitted where it does not affect the point at hand. Thus, for example, the lexical specification for *met* must be elaborated to permit examples such as *the boys met*, etc.

[6] In fact, the general filtering device (53) can be dispensed with altogether if we define the phrases of the language to include all those that receive a "complete" interpretation. It then follows that incompletely interpreted strings are not phrases of the language. For convenience, (53) is retained throughout this essay.

[7] It should be noted that the following example is somewhat deviant.

(i)   ?John, who I wanted to see and I did, is my friend.

However, this example clearly has a different feel from (103b). It is not the interaction property that rings untrue of (i), but rather the head property, for (ii) seems to be equally deviant.

(ii)   ?John, who I wanted to see and I did see, is my friend.

It is generally the case that if one conjoined sentence is headed by some complementizer element, then both must be so headed, as illustrated below.

(iii)   a. ?I know that John ate udon and Mary drank kumiss.

     b. ?John realizes that you are smart and Mary is not so smart.

     c. ?Do you know whether he left or Mary arrived?

It should be noted, however, that there may well be speakers who accept such examples, the point being, that such speakers reject (103b). Incidentally, some examples which violate the head constraint strike me as more acceptable, including example (63) from Bresnan.

REFERENCES

Brame, M. K. 1976. *Conjectures and Refutations in Syntax and Semantics*. Elsevier-North Holland Publishing Co., New York.

Brame, M. K. 1978a. *Base Generated Syntax*. Noit Amrofer Publishing Co. P.O. Box 15176, Seattle, Wa. 98115.

Brame, M. K. 1978b. Discourse and Binding without Transformations. *Linguistic Analysis* 4: 365–404.

Brame, M. K. 1978c. The Base Hypothesis and the Spelling Prohibition. *Linguistic Analysis* 4: 1–30.

Brame, M. K. 1979. Chomsky/Lasnik Filters Are Special Cases of Functional Deviance. Paper delivered at 1979 Sloan Foundation Workshop at Stanford. In this volume.

Brame, M. K. 1979. (to appear a). *Linguistic Problems* (23 linguistic problems discussed with proposed solutions)

Brame, M. K. 1978 (to appear b). Lexical Phonology.

Bresnan, J. 1972. Theory of Complementation in English Syntax. MIT doctoral dissertation.

Bresnan, J. 1976. On the Form and Functioning of Transformations. *Linguistic Inquiry* 7: 3–40.

Bresnan, J. 1977. Variables in the Theory of Transformations. In *Formal Syntax*, ed. by Culicover, Wasow, and Akmajian.

Bresnan, J. 1978. A Realistic Transformational Grammar. In *Linguistic Theory and Psychological Reality*, ed. by Halle, Bresnan, and Miller.

Chomsky, N. 1957. *Syntactic Structures*. The Hague: Mouton.

Chomsky, N. 1968. *Language and Mind*. Harcourt, Brace, and World.

Chomsky, N. 1977. On WH-Movement. In *Formal Syntax*. Ed. by Culicover, Wasow, and Akmajian.

Chomsky, N. and H. Lasnik 1977. Filters and Control. *Linguistic Inquiry* 8: 425–504.

DeCarrico, J. 1978. Anaphoric Relations of Indefinites. U. of Wa. unpublished.

Emonds, J. 1976. *A Transformational Approach to English Syntax*. Academic Press.

Guerssel, M. 1977. Constraints on Phonological Rules. *Linguistic Analysis* 3: 267–305.

Guerssel, M. 1978. A Condition on Assimilation Rules. *Linguistic Analysis* 4: 225–254.

Lakoff, G. 1976. Pronouns and Reference. In *Syntax and Semantics* 7.

Lasnik, H. 1976. Remarks on Coreference. *Linguistic Analysis* 2: 1–22.

Lasnik, H. and R. Fiengo 1974. Complement Object Deletion. *Linguistic Inquiry* 5: 535–571.

Reinhart, T. 1976. *The Syntactic Domain of Anaphora*. MIT doctoral dissertation.

Ross, J. 1967. *Constraints on Variables in Syntax*. MIT doctoral dissertation.

Sag, I. 1976. *Deletion and Logical Form*. MIT doctoral dissertation.

Schachter, P. 1978. Propredicates. *Linguistic Analysis* 4:187–224.

Wasow, T. 1972. *Anaphoric Relations in English*. MIT doctoral dissertation.

Wasow, T. 1977. Review of *Conjectures and Refutations in Syntax and Semantics*. *Linguistic Analysis* 3:377–395.

Williams, E. 1977. Discourse and Logical Form. *Linguistic Inquiry* 8: 101–139.

Woolford, E. (to appear) Topicalization and Clefting without WH-Movement. Paper presented at NELS VIII.

Yildirim, C. 1978. *A Functional Interpretive Approach to Turkish*. University of Washington doctoral dissertation.

CHOMSKY/LASNIK FILTERS

ARE SPECIAL CASES OF FUNCTIONAL DEVIANCE

Sensei, do they really miss this parallelism?

>   *It is unclear *what John to do*.
>   *It bothers me *Bill to win*.
>   *It came as a surprise to me *John was here*.

>   It is unclear *what to do*.
>   It bothers me *for Bill to win*.
>   It came as a surprise to me *that John was here*.

Yes, gakusei, they do.

1. Introduction
2. Unexpressed Generalization
3. Functional Deviance
4. The Controversial Examples
5. A Hitherto Missed Syntactic Generalization
6. Lexical Integrity
7. Extraposition and Gapping as Anaphora
8. The Missing Subject Problem
9. *for-for* and *for-to*
10. Infinitival Constructions
11. Conclusion
   Notes
   References

CHOMSKY/LASNIK FILTERS

ARE SPECIAL CASES OF FUNCTIONAL DEVIANCE

1. INTRODUCTION

Do the following examples really pose a dilemma for linguistic theory?

(1) a. *The man met you is my friend.
     b. *He left is a surprise.

They do for Chomsky/Lasnik (1978). Before discussing the reasons behind the Chomsky/Lasnik concern for such examples, let us take a fresh look at (1a) and (1b) in the absence of theoretical bias. A gut response to such cases runs as follows: It is possible to interpret *the man met you* in (1a) as a sentential proposition and it is possible to interpret *is my friend* in the same example as a tensed predicate. But that is as far as we can go. It is simply impossible to compose the two because sentences do not select for tensed predicates and tensed predicates do not select for complementizerless subjects. Nor does the predicate *met* select for a tensed predicate in addition to its direct object argument. Hence, it is simply not possible to provide an interpretation for (1a).

Likewise, in the case of (1b), we can interpret *he left* as a sentential proposition and *is a surprise* as a tensed predicate, but again we are at a loss to compose the two.

It seems that this is precisely what a good theory of language should say about these examples: they are deviant for failure to allow composibility of their parts. Let us call this kind of deviance *functional deviance*. Before turning to a more explicit characterization of functional deviance, let us first consider several additional examples.

Examples such as the following have been adduced in the literature, cf. Chomsky (1971, 1973).

(2) a. *John is believed is hungry.
     b. John is believed to be hungry.

67

Again, common sense tells us that *John is believed* and *is hungry* in (2a) can each be interpreted but cannot be composed. The predicate *believed* simply does not select a tensed predicate as *argument*. By contrast, infinitive phrases can function as arguments and in this case *believed* does select for this type of argument. Hence the parts of (2b) are composable and the example can be interpreted.

We see that there is a generalization to be expressed here in connection with examples such as (1a), (1b), and (2a). All should be out for the same reason.

Indeed, all of the filters proposed by Chomsky and Lasnik are special cases of functional deviance. But this is perhaps not so easy to see when one is working within a framework such as transformational grammar as opposed to a framework within which one works directly off the surface.

Now what is Chomsky and Lasnik's account of (1a) and (1b)? To account for such examples, they propose the following filter.

(3)   *[$_{NP}$ NP tense VP]

Filter (3) stipulates that all NP's comprised of NP plus tensed predicates are marked as deviant, where the deviance is indicated by an asterisk. This account strikes the uninitiated reader as somewhat puzzling, for, after all, *the man met you* in (1a) and *he left* in (1b) are interpreted as S's, not NP's. However, the uneasiness may well recede if we could only agree with an underlying assumption—that (1a) and (1b) derive from a more abstract underlying representation with complementizers such as *who* and *that*, as indicated below.

(4)   a. [the man who met you] is my friend
      b. [that he left] is a surprise

If one could buy (4), then perhaps it would be possible to accept the filter (3), for Chomsky and Lasnik claim that there is a rule which freely deletes complementizer elements. The trouble here is that no evidence is provided for a rule of complementizer deletion. Chomsky and Lasnik simply assume the existence of such a rule and pursue its consequences.

Perhaps if we forego the latter assumption, the problems entailed by the examples in (1) will go away. We could then do without the ad hoc filter. After all, the rule of free complementizer deletion does violate the Spelling Prohibition which is supported by a good deal of evidence, cf. Brame (1978a). But even if we do not adopt a rule of free complementizer deletion, a problem arises nevertheless, in the form expressed from the outset; namely, when *the man met you* and *he left* in (1a) and (1b) are bracketed with S, instead of NP, we must still account for the deviance of the complete examples given.

It should even be granted that the filter (3) leads to a loss of generalization, for it fails to generalize to the situation just alluded to. A second principle would be needed to cover such a situation and whether this principle involves phrase structure rules, lexical insertion, a new filter, or whatever, such a principle will differ from the filter (3).

It would not be unreasonable, therefore, to abandon the free deletion rule once and for all and with it the filter given in (3), attempting instead to provide a general account of (1a) and (1b) in terms of functional deviance.

This conclusion becomes even more obvious when we turn to (2a) where a simple comparison shows that there is indeed a generalization underlying this example and (1a)–(1b).

The problem of accounting for (2) was originally posed by Chomsky, who considered the deviance of (2a) to be related to the passive transformation. Thus, it was suggested that (2a) was derived from (5a), and that (2b) was derived from (5b).

(5) a. Someone believes John is hungry.
     b. Someone believes John to be hungry.

Chomsky's question was this: Why does the passive transformation apply to (5b) to yield (2b), but not to (5a) to yield (5b)? His answer was: ". . . let us propose the principle that nothing can be extracted from a tensed sentence" (1971, p. 34). This new principle became known as the Tensed Sentence Condition [TSC] and later, after counterexamples began to appear, as the Propositional Island Constraint [PIC].

Now it has been noted repeatedly that the deviance of (2a) has nothing to do with the passive transformation per se, cf. Brame (1977, 1978b). For example, it has been noted that the following examples are deviant where they have nothing to do with passive.

(6) a. *John believes is hungry.
     b. *Mary believed were hungry.

It is obvious that these examples have nothing to do with passive and that therefore TSC cannot provide an account of their deviance. It is equally obvious that a general account of these examples should extend to the problematic example adduced by Chomsky in (2a). My contention is that this account should also extend to all of the examples for which Chomsky and Lasnik propose a host of ad hoc filters. And this account is founded on a more lexically based theory of syntax.

2. UNEXPRESSED GENERALIZATIONS

Let us briefly review the alleged motivation for the Chomsky/Lasnik approach to complementizers in English. They are intent on relating the following examples.

(7)   a. the man that I saw
      b. the man who(m) I saw
      c. the man I saw

All of these examples involve well-formed relative clause constructions. In an attempt to relate such examples, Chomsky and Lasnik propose a single underlying deep structure such as (8a), where *that* is spelled out, in conjunction with a rule of *wh*-movement which gives rise to (8b).

(8)   a. the man [that [I saw who(m)]]
      b. the man [who(m) that [I saw t]]

To (8b) the following rule of free deletion is applicable.

(9)   In the domain COMP, delete $[_\alpha \varphi]$, where α is an arbitrary category and φ an arbitrary structure.

Rule (9) permits deletion of any element dominated by COMP. This rule, then, provides for all three examples in (7). In the case of (7a), only *who(m)* is deleted. In (7b), only *that* is deleted, and in (7c), both *who(m)* and *that* have been deleted.

There is a problem with this analysis. Since the deletion rule (9) is optional, it need not apply to (8b), which results in the following ungrammatical example.

(10)   *the man who(m) that I saw

To compensate for this unwanted result, a special filter is proposed.

(11)   *$[_{COMP}wh$-phrase $\varphi]$, $\varphi \neq$ e

Now we must ask: Is (11) simply an ad hoc consequence of a bad analysis or is there in fact some independent motivation for it? The answer to this question turns out to relate to the former possibility. To see this it will be necessary to proceed to additional examples.

In fact, we have already seen that further ad hoc theoretical consequences inhere in the Chomsky/Lasnik approach. Thus, pursuing this analysis, we have a deep structure such as (12a) below, which is converted to (12b) by wh-movement and subsequently to the ungrammatical (12c) by rule (9).

(12)   a.   the man [that [who met you]] is my friend
       b.   the man [who that [t met you]] is my friend
       c.   *the man met you is my friend

As noted in section 1, this result makes additional theoretical elaboration necessary, namely filter (3).

At this point I think it is necessary to seriously consider the possibility that the two filters, (3) and (11), are simply ad hoc consequences of a faulty analysis. Certainly a shadow will have been cast over the whole undertaking if additional devices are a consequence of the analysis involving deletion of material in COMP.

There is further evidence which does show that the proposed analysis is faulty. Consider the following example.

(13)   the man to whom John spoke

This example will derive from (14a) by wh-movement and deletion of *that*, as indicated in (14b) and (14c).

(14)   a. the man [that [John spoke to whom]]
       b. the man [to whom that [John spoke]]
       c. the man [to whom [John spoke]]

The problem that now arises is this. Since the material in COMP is freely deletable by (9), we could delete *whom* in both (14b) and (14c) to derive the ungrammatical examples presented below.

(15)   a. *the man to that John spoke
       b. *the man to John spoke

Now what ad hoc device is summoned to fix up this consequence of the analysis? Here Chomsky and Lasnik invoke A/A holding of the deletion rule.

(16)   "We assume that this is excluded by the A/A Condition holding of [9], since these elements, taken as members of the category α, are included in larger elements of some category (α being arbitrary)."
       [p. 446]

It would be a mistake to concede that A/A is independently motivated and that therefore its application to (14b) and (14c) involves no additional complication in the grammar. In the first place, we have no idea of what precisely A/A is. The principle has not been precisely formulated and it has been unclear just what motivation is accorded A/A in light of Chomsky's adoption of subjacency, Specified Subject Condition, and Tensed S Condition, etc. Until and unless the full range of evidence for and against A/A is supplied, together with a precise formulation of the principle, no "independent motivation" can be conceded. Moreover, there is every reason to believe that A/A simply leads to a further loss of generalization in this case. Thus, (15a) and (15b) are blocked by A/A holding of deletion in COMP. But the following examples will be out for totally different reasons.

(17)   a. *the man to that John saw
       b. *the man to John saw

Now it is not A/A that would rule out (17a) and (17b) within the Chomsky/Lasnik theory. Rather it would be lexical subcategorization, since the verb *see* does not select a prepositional phrase. Hence the situation could not arise which would allow the prepositional phrase to be moved to the COMP position which would in turn be susceptible to deletion by (9), blocked by A/A. In other words, one principle, A/A, is invoked to rule out (15a) and (15b), while a second distinct principle, subcategorization, is invoked to rule out (17a) and (17b). It would be nice, however, if the same general device could be utilized to rule out both (15) and (17). The theory which will be advocated here does in fact allow for the generalization.

Are there yet further ad hoc consequences of the Chomsky/Lasnik approach? There are. Since elements in COMP are freely deletable by (9), we may apply it to the complete prepositional phrase *to whom* in (14b) and (14c) and thereby derive the following examples.

(18)   a. *the man that John spoke
       b. *the man John spoke

Or consider example (19a). Rule (9) could apply to delete *of whom* to yield ungrammatical (19b).

(19)   a. the boy pictures of whom John took
       b. *the boy pictures John took

What new principle must be invoked to avoid these bad results? Here Chomsky and Lasnik invoke the alleged principle of recoverability of deletion.

(20)   "We assume that this possibility is excluded by the recoverability principle for deletion ... items from the lexicon cannot be deleted unless they are explicitly mentioned in the deletion rule. Since the contents of the *wh*-phrases [in (14b), (14c), (19a)] include lexical material, these phrases cannot be deleted."   [pp. 446–7]

Again, an apparently old principle is drawn on to account for the unwanted consequences of the proposed theory, a free ride. But once again, "independent motivation" cannot be granted since no explicit formulation of the principle is ever provided. Moreover, as Chomsky and Lasnik note, there is an inconsistency involved in (20). If lexical material cannot be deleted by rule (9) since it is not explicitly mentioned in rule (9), then *who(m)* should not be deletable in (7b) to ultimately yield (7c). To overcome this inconsistency, Chomsky and Lasnik remark:

(21)   "There is a residual semantic content in relative pronouns, namely the feature Human ... But this (or any) residual semantic content is redundant, since it is expressed in the head of the construction. We assume that an appropriate concept of recoverability will be restricted to lexical items, ignoring such redundant features." [p. 447, fn. 46]

We see then that yet a further device is needed to account for an additional unwanted consequence of the proposed theory. Let us now tabulate these results. The following theoretical devices are proposed as a consequence of very simple relative clause constructions.

(22) a. Free deletion in COMP, rule (9)
      b. Filter (3), an ad hoc consequence of (12c)
      c. Filter (11), an ad hoc consequence of (10)
      d. A/A, an ad hoc consequence of (15)
      e. Recoverability of Deletion, an ad hoc consequence of (18), (19b)

Now it will be clear to unbiased observers that something is indeed missed in connection with the theory which must summon this range of ad hoc devices to account for unwanted results which are a consequence of the theory. Perhaps we can do better and go on to account for the generalization underlying (15) and (17) and the generalization underlying the examples discussed in section 1, repeated below in (23).

(23) a. *The man met you is my friend.
      b. *John is believed is hungry.
      c. *John believes is hungry.

Recall that the Chomsky/Lasnik approach involves the following devices to account for (23).

(24) a. Filter (3)
      b. Tensed S Condition
      c. Phrase Structure, Lexicon, etc.

It would be desirable to express the generalization underlying (23 a–c) and to be able to dispense with ad hoc devices such as the Tensed S Condition, the proliferation of filters of the Chomsky/Lasnik type, Recoverability of Deletion, A/A, and in fact, all of the constraints and conditions proposed within the framework of transformational grammar. There is in fact some hope that this objective can be realized. In this particular case, all of (23 a–c), in addition to other examples discussed in this section and many examples adduced by Chomsky and Lasnik, turn out to be examples which are functionally deviant and incomplete in the sense to be elucidated in the following section.

3. FUNCTIONAL DEVIANCE

Before sketching out an analysis which can express the generalizations uncovered in the previous sections, let us review the relevant examples and provide a naive idea of what is to be accomplished. Relevant examples include the following.

(25) a. *The man met you is my friend.
      b. *John is believed is hungry.
      c. *John believes is hungry.
      d. *the man who(m) that I saw
      e. *the man to that John spoke
      f. *the boy pictures John took

The basic idea is that expressed in section 1. We might look at all these examples as concatenated lexical words. We attempt to build up syntactic interpretations, employing rules of composition, which ultimately hinge on the functional structure of the lexical items in question. In all of the examples listed in (25) something goes wrong and a functionally complete interpretation cannot be derived.

Consider example (25a). Here we can build up a syntactic interpretation for *the man met you* and *is my friend*, but the two cannot be composed. Similarly, it is not possible to compose *John is believed* and *is hungry* in (25b). Again, in the case of (25c), *John believes* and *is hungry* cannot be composed, and in the case of (25d), *who(m)* and *that I saw* cannot be composed. Similarly, there is no way to compose *to*, which selects an NP and *that John spoke*, which is not an NP. And finally (25f) represents an example for which it is not possible to compose the parts with *pictures*.

The idea to be pursued here is that when such a situation arises where the various parts of a string cannot be provided a complete syntactic interpretation, then that string is functionally deviant with respect to the attempted interpretation. The string is not a phrase in the language. Let us now turn to a sketch of such a theory.

To express the generalization mentioned above, it is necessary to forego all transformations. Although it is possible to base generate most of the constructions of interest, cf. Brame (1976, 1978b), Bresnan (1978), here I will be working directly off the surface. It will no longer be possible to simply gloss over lexical specifications, since, as we shall see, the functional structure associated with lexical specifications plays an intimate role in the interpretive process.

By way of providing an introduction to the approach advocated here, let us provide partial lexical specifications for words such as *the, man, met, you,* and *John*.

(26)   the; D, __(N)
(27)   man; N
(28)   met; V, __NP^o
(29)   you; NP^x
(30)   John; NP^y

Lexical entries consist of two components, a phonological specification comprising the initial component, and a functional or syntactic specification comprising the second component, which will be called the functional structure of the word in question. Superscripts in lexical specifications can be taken to indicate a range of information, including grammatical function, number, gender, etc. Here I will simplify and take the superscript to indicate grammatical function alone. Thus, in (29) and (30) we see that *you* and *John* function as NP arguments which vary according to their function as subject, object, etc. By contrast, an NP such as *I*, for example, must be specified lexically as a subject NP, viz. NP^s. The actual function of *you* and *John* may be determined within a given syntactic context and several rules to effect this identification will be provided below.

It should be noted that lexical words exhibit two basic types, arguments and functions, and an adequate notation should reflect this distinction. Thus, arguments such as *you* and *John* and *man* have simple functional structures, whereas functions such as *the*, *met*, etc. have complex functional structures, consisting of an initial segment and a context. The context represents the argument structure selected by the function word. It should be noted that functions, like arguments, also reflect grammatical function and should also be superscripted, but for simplicity these details are omitted here. A more adequate (but still impoverished) notation is provided in Brame (1978b, 1979).

The basic syntax is provided by a general concatenation operator, which gives rise to strings of concatenated initial components of lexical entries, as provided below.

(31)   the man met you
(32)   the met you John man

We now wish to provide a means of building up a complete interpretation for (31), while at the same time failing to provide a complete interpretation for (32). To this end the following rules of composition are proposed.

(33) Rules of Composition

 a. For each phonological word a, compose a as some cateogory B.

 b. Compose $\overset{\frown}{A}\ \overset{\frown}{B_1\ B_2}\ ...\ \overset{\frown}{B_n}$ as the complete second component of the lexical specification of A, where A is a function term and B_i is an argument term, $0 \le i \le n$.

Applying (14a) to (12), we obtain the following.

(34)

D	N	V	NP^x
the	man	met	you

The variable superscript x, indicating the grammatical function of NP arguments, can be identified by rules which make reference to the position of the NP in the concatenated string. For example, subject and object can be expressed by rules such as the following.

(35) $\quad NP^x \rightarrow \begin{cases} NP^s & / & \_\_V \\ NP^o & / & V\_\_ \end{cases}$

Thus, the x corresponding to *you* in (34) will be filled in as o, indicating the *you* functions as an object noun phrase argument.

 We now apply (33b) and obtain the following.

(36)

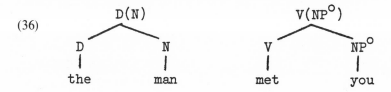

It is assumed that the following equivalences hold.

(37) $D(N) \equiv NP^x$
   $V(...) \equiv VP$
   $VP(NP^s) \equiv S$

Thus, (36) is equivalent to the following, where s is supplied by (35).

(38)

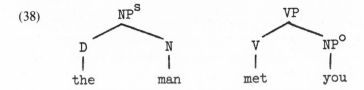

In general, examples such as (36) and (38) will be written as follows.

(39)

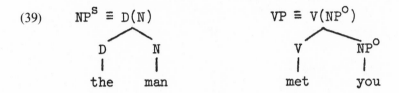

Since VP is a function term, we now wish to compose it with its argument NP^s. This can be accomplished with the following rule; it is also assumed that the equivalence VP(NP^s) ≡ S is to be added to (37).

(40)   Compose NP^s VP as VP(NP^s)

Applying (40) to (39), we obtain the following.

(41)

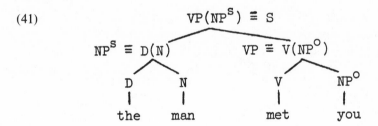

We now wish to check (41) for well-formedness. This involves an indexing procedure such as the following.

(42)   a. Let T be a term dominating a lexical category *a*. If (a; T, ...)ϵ Lexicon, then assign T a distinct index *i*, written T : *i*.

   b. Let T be a term directly dominating terms A B$_1$ B$_2$ ... B$_n$. Then substitute the indices of the latter for corresponding terms in the equivalence of T.

   c. If T ≡ A(B$_1$ ... B$_n$) and every term in the latter is indexed, then index T.

Applying the indexing procedure to (41), we obtain the following.

(43)
$$S \equiv VP(NP^S):h(k) = p$$

$$NP^S \equiv D(N):f(i) = k \qquad VP \equiv V(NP^O):g(j) = h$$

D:f	N:i	V:g	NP^O:j
the	man	met	you

It can be seen that all of the relevant functional structure in (43) has been indexed. We shall refer to the collection of all such index structures at the root of a phrase as an interpretation of that phrase. Thus, an interpretation of the phrase *the man met you* is the following.

(44) p = h(k) = (g(j))(k) = h((f(i)) = (g(j))(f(i)), where f = *the*, i = *man*, etc.

With this background it is now possible to define incompleteness.

(45) Incompleteness

A string $a_1 \dots a_n$ is incomplete with respect to an interpretation φ provided there is a term T in φ corresponding to no index or provided there is no index in φ corresponding to a_i for some i, $1 \le i \le n$.

A string is said to be completely interpreted with respect to an interpretation φ provided the string is not incomplete. In the case of our example, *the man met you* is complete with respect to the interpretation provided in (44). Of course the same example may well be incomplete with respect to a different interpretation, where the interpretive procedures were applied in a way incompatible with the result given in (43). It is therefore important to bear in mind that incompleteness as provided in (45) is a relative notion. We may now define functional deviance as follows.

(46) Functional Deviance

A string $a_1 \dots a_n$ is functionally deviant if it is incomplete under all interpretations.

The example provided in (32) is functionally deviant in the sense of (46).

There is simply no way to compose all its parts so as to be assigned a single index p.

4. THE CONTROVERSIAL EXAMPLES

Let us now return to examples such as (25a), repeated below as (47).

(47)   *The man met you is my friend.

It should be clear that this example is deviant with respect to any attempted interpretation. A complete interpretation can be provided for *the man met you* as well as for *is my friend*, but there are no provisions for composing the resulting S and VP terms to yield a reading for the complete string in (47). Consequently, as a single phrase, (47) is incomplete.
   This is also true of example (25b), repeated below as (48).

(48)   *John is believed is hungry.

We can take *believed* to be a lexical word. Like many passive participles, *believed* selects an optional agentive phrase argument, but never a VP function. Hence, we are unable to compose *John is believed* and *is hungry* so as to provide ultimately an index for the complete string in (48). It follows that this example too is functionally deviant.
   Precisely the same consequence holds for example (25c), repeated below as (49).

(49)   *John believes is hungry.

The phrase *is hungry* is not an argument term, but rather a function. The lexical item *believe* is specified to select various types of arguments, for example, NP arguments, sentential arguments, but never VP functions. Hence, *John believes* and *is hungry* cannot be composed and consequently example (49) is incomplete.
   We see that all three examples are generalized within the proposed framework, whereas they are treated differently within the Chomsky/ Lasnik framework. Since example (47) is ruled out on grounds of incompleteness, it follows that filters such as (3) are not needed. Such a filter is simply a special case of incompleteness, and not a very interesting one at that. But this is also true of other examples. Thus, there is no reason for adopting a filter to rule out (11), repeated here as (25d).

(50)   *the man who(m) that I saw

The lexical item *who* selects a sentential argument S, not an $\bar{S}$ argument. It thus follows that *who(m)* and *that I saw* in (50) will not be properly composed to permit indexing to proceed in terms of Operator Binding, cf. Brame (1978). As a consequence, (50) will be functionally deviant. The net result is that the proposed filter (11) is unneeded. It is simply a special ad hoc instance of functional deviance, and again not a very interesting one.

Again, in the case of (15a) and (15b), repeated below as (51), we encounter examples which are functionally deviant.

(51)   a. *the man to that John spoke
       b. *the man to John spoke

The lexical item *to* selects an object of preposition NP argument. In neither of (51) will this lexical restriction be satisfied so that proper indexing can be assigned to yield an interpretation for the complete strings. Hence these examples too are incomplete.

Now let us return to the examples provided in (17), repeated below as (52).

(52)   a. *the man to that John saw
       b. *the man to John saw

Recall that these examples will be ruled out by completely different mechanisms than the A/A principle ruling out (15a) and (15b). In section 2, however, I asserted that they should be out for the same reason. Now it is easy to see that in fact (52a) and (52b) are out for the same reason, namely, *to* cannot be composed with *that John saw* or *John saw* to permit proper indexing. Thus, the generalization can be expressed within the proposed framework.

Now consider examples such as (18a) and (18b), repeated below as (53).

(53)   a. *the man that John spoke
       b. *the man John spoke

These examples, recall, would be derived under the Chomsky/Lasnik analysis, which, as noted above, occasions a new principle, Recoverability of Deletion. However, these examples are functionally deviant under the analysis I am advocating. To see this, it is necessary to provide a lexical specification for the word _that_. It can be provided a lexical specification with a multiple functional structure relating to its complementizer and relative functions.

(54)   that; C, __(S) or NP^x, F^{rel}(__)(S)

According to (54), _that_ can function as either a true complementizer introducing sentential arguments or else as a relative pronoun which is an operator suffix of the relative operator $F^{rel}(NP^x)$, as in Brame (1978b). Let us now consider the following well-formed pair.

(55)   a. the man that John met
       b. the man John met

The following interpretations can be built up for _the man_ and _that John met_, respectively.

(56) NP^x : i   where i = _the man_
       $(F^{rel}(NP^x))((V(NP^o))(NP^s))$: $F^{rel}(x)((f(NP^o))(j))$
       where x = _that_, f = _met_, j = _John_

To (56) Operator Binding applies, identifying x with NP^o and indexing the prefix F^{rel}, whereupon x is linked to the lexical head index i by a rule of anaphora. The net result is that (55a) receives a complete interpretation. (Note that there is no rule of extraposition from NP since such a rule is replaced with the rule of anaphora linking the relative pronoun with the index of the lexical head.)[1]

The same result holds for (55b) provided we posit a rule which will ensure that Operator Binding applies. Such a rule would have the effect of inserting a relative operator $F^{rel}(NP^x)$ just in case an NP is adjacent to an S, as follows.

(57) ϕ → $F^{rel}(NP^x)$ /   NP__S

By anaphora the operator suffix NP^x will again be identified with the lexical head index and Operator Binding will ensue, providing for a complete interpretation. This analysis automatically explains the following range of data.

(58) a. the gun that I bought went off
 b. the gun which I bought went off
 c. the gun I bought went off
 d. the gun went off that I bought
 e. the gun went off which I bought
 f. *the gun went off I bought

Example (58f) cannot be provided a single index because it is not possible to link *I bought* with anything preceding it since rule (57) is inapplicable. Also it is not possible to identify the object argument of *bought* since Operator Binding will be inapplicable. Hence (58f) is functionally deviant.

This analysis will also explain the following distinctions.

(59) a. the man that I talked with
 b. the man who(m) I talked with
 c. the man I talked with
 d. the man with whom I talked
 e. *the man with that I talked

Because *that* is not lexically specified for the relevant complex functional structure, it follows that (59e) will not receive a complete interpretation. By contrast *whom* is provided the following partial lexical specification.

(60)   whom; NP^x, $F^{rel}((P(\_)))(S)$

Of course, for those speakers who employ the prescriptive dialect as opposed to the formal dialect, i.e. allowing *whom* in (59b) instead of the natural *who*, (60) must be complicated, cf. Brame (1978b, fn. 7). Others, who speak the modern dialect do not include *whom* anywhere in their lexicon, from which it follows that examples such as (59d) are not possible.

Let us now return to the examples provided in (53). It is easy to see that these examples can be provided variable indices for the relative pronoun and it is equally clear that Operator Binding will not be applicable. This follows from the fact that *spoke* selects a PP argument whereas *that* functions as an NP argument, not as a PP argument. It follows that the conditions associated with Operator Binding are not fulfilled, cf. Brame (1978b), and consequently we are left with a functionally deviant string. This implies that we can do without the recoverability of deletion principle which Chomsky and Lasnik must employ. In sum, the generalization can be expressed within the proposed analysis. Within the framework of the filtering approach, it cannot.

All of the ad hoc devices listed in (22), and others besides, can be eliminated when we view matters in the light of incompleteness. Each and every phonological word has its associated functional specification. If rules of composition apply so as to appropriately compose these words to allow indexing of the root, we will derive a complete interpretation. Otherwise we will be left with a functionally deviant example. All of the deviant examples discussed by Chomsky and Lasnik which they claim occasion a number of filters are treated in a straightforward manner in terms of incompleteness. Indeed filters can be viewed as special cases of functional deviance.

5. A HITHERTO MISSED SYNTACTIC GENERALIZATION

There is a general feature of the analysis advocated here which is not a property of syntactic theories such as transformational grammar. Transformational grammar is a theory of sentence grammar and is, as such, unnecessarily restrictive. This fact has important consequences, for it gives rise to a new ad hoc filter. By contrast, the theory advocated here is a theory of syntactic phrasal types, including sentences as only one of the wide variety of syntactic types. The following are all well-formed syntactic types.

(61) a. met Mary
      b. with a knife
      c. John met Mary
      d. that John saw
      e. whether Mary ate the apple
      f. John asked whether Mary ate the apple

The theory advocated here allows for the interpretation of finer syntactic types than S's. Thus, in the case of (61a), for example, *met Mary* can be provided a complete interpretation qua VP, but, of course, not as S. Similarly, *with a knife* in (61b) can be provided a complete interpretation qua PP, given appropriate lexical specifications, but not as S. In (61c), *John met Mary* can be provided a complete interpretation as S, but not as VP or PP. Now, examples (61d) and (61e) are like (61a) and (61b) in that they can be provided complete interpretations which are not S, but rather finer syntactic types. But, clearly, (61d) and (61e) are not ungrammatical. They are complete as $\overline{S}$, as opposed to S.

We readily see that because transformational grammar views syntax in a distorted way, special devices must be invented to rule out (61d) and (61e). Chomsky and Lasnik propose the following filter.

(62)   *[$_{\overline{S}}$ COMP NP ...], where $\overline{S}$ is a root sentence

Chomsky and Lasnik claim that (62) implies that deletion of *that* by rule (62) is obligatory. In fact, the filter (62) is simply an ad hoc consequence of failing to view grammar in the general way which has been suggested above, i.e. as a theory of syntactic types, not as a theory of sentence grammar. Examples such as (61d) and (61e) are no more deviant than are the phrasal types in (61a) and (61b), or, for that matter, than the sentences in (61c) and (61f).

Not only is it possible to formulate the theory to encompass finer syntactic types than S, we can go on to provide for coarser syntactic relations, including, for example, the question/answer relation, the theme/topic, relation, and others. Some preliminary work along these lines is provided in Brame (1978c).

In conclusion, yet another filter can be dispensed with when syntax is viewed in a nontransformational framework such as that advocated here. This is again a welcome result since we are always interested in dispensing with excess theoretical machinery. Unlike the previous examples discussed, however, the crucial examples here are not deviant, in spite of claims to the contrary in terms of (62).

6. LEXICAL INTEGRITY

Let us now return to the Chomsky/Lasnik approach and in particular to filter (3). Recall that a range of ad hoc devices, listed in (22), are required to force through the analysis involving free deletion of elements in COMP. There are, however, additional problems that accrue to the analysis. Thus, the following examples are cited in the Chomsky/Lasnik paper.

(63)   a.   the fact that John was here surprised me
       b.   *the fact John was here surprised me
(64)   a.   it came as a surprise to me that John was here
       b.   *it came as a surprise to me John was here

(65) a. it is unlikely that John is here
     b. *it is unlikely John is here
(66) a. I pleaded with Bill that he shouldn't hire her
     b. *I pleaded with Bill he shouldn't hire her
(67) a. John believes (that) Mary saw Sam, and Bill, that Sue saw Harry
     b. *John believes (that) Mary saw Sam, and Bill, Sue saw Harry

The deviant (b) examples result from applying rule (9) within the Chomsky/Lasnik framework. Once again, we see that the analysis raises more questions than it answers. New complications are needed to cover the (b) examples, and these complications amount to a redescription of the problems themselves. The complication is incorporated into filter (3) under the disguised assertion that filter (3) "is insufficiently general" [p. 484], as given below.

(68) *[αNP tense VP], unless α is adjacent to and in the domain of [+V], *that*, or NP

I think it is clear that this "generalized" version of (3) is in fact a complication. The true ad hoc nature of (68) becomes readily apparent when Chomsky and Lasnik recognize that (68) predicts that examples which are similar to their old example (1a) are predicted to be grammatical. Such examples differ from (1a) only in that the complement is adjacent to [+V], as indicated below.

(69) *I saw the man met you   ⇐ I saw the man (who, that) met you

The "generalized" filter (68) predicts that (69) is grammatical since the putative complement *the man met you* is adjacent to and in the domain of a verb, i.e. [+V], after deletion of the complementizer elements. To correct for this additional flaw, the more complex filter (70) is proposed.

(70) *[αNP tense VP], unless α ≠ NP and is adjacent to and in the domain of [+F], *that*, or NP

There can be little doubt. Filter (70) is not a generalization in any natural sense of that term. It indicates, once again, that something has been missed.

There is an extremely telling criticism of the Chomsky/Lasnik approach which goes to the heart of their dilemma. This involves their change of [+V] in (68) to [+F] in (70). What is the reason for this alteration? The answer lies in examples such as the following.

(71) a. Bill wondered that Dennis was such an outstanding guard.
      b. *Bill wondered Dennis was such an outstanding guard.
(72) a. I am sad that you don't understand.
      b. *I am sad you don't understand.
          cf. I am glad you don't understand.
(73) a. She demanded that he leave.
      b. *She demanded he leave.

Chomsky and Lasnik recognize that many predicates do not allow free deletion of *that*, although they claim that deletion of *that* is "fairly free" [p. 486]. Statistics are clearly irrelevant. We must ask just how they would account for the deviance of the (b) examples in (71)–(73). What they do is posit an abstract feature F, which they take to be a "subfeature of [+V]" and include F in (70), assuming that F "characterizes verbs and adjectives that permit the structure resulting from deletion of *that*."

This particular maneuver reveals quite clearly that Chomsky and Lasnik are attempting to transfer truly lexical phenomena to the domain of filters, a move which is reminiscent of the generative semantics attempt to force lexical phenomena into the domain of transformations, cf. Brame (1976, Part I). As they note, whether or not a verb requires a *that* complementizer is to some extent "erratic", but they fail to note that the lexicon is traditionally the repository of erratic and idiosyncratic properties of lexical items, as emphasized by Chomsky himself in earlier work. Once this is realized, it becomes evident that the presence or absence of *that* should in fact be expressed in the lexicon as part of the argument structure associated with the verbs and adjectives in question, including perhaps other items, such as modals, cf. Bresnan (1972). Thus, *that* itself should be a lexical item and should be available for selection. The example listed in (73b) is another example of an incompletely interpreted string, where the argument structure of *demand* is not satisfied, implying that *she demanded* and *he leave* cannot be composed so as to be appropriately indexed. Thus, *demanded he leave* is out for very much the same reason as *with he leave*, as indicated in (74).

(74) a. *demanded he leave
      b. *with he leave

In both cases, we are left with incompletely interpreted results. The lexical item *demand* selects an $\overline{S}$ argument, not an S argument. The lexical item *with* selects an NP argument, not an S argument.

By failing to recognize that complementizers are lexical items on a par with other function words, Chomsky and Lasnik fail to note generalizations such as those indicated in (74) and completely miss the parallelism between the following sets of examples.

(75) a. that *John left*   assumes *John left*
      b. *that *to leave*   *assumes *to leave*

In (75) we see that the function words *that* and *assumes* are similar in that both select an S argument, but not a $\overline{VP}$ argument. This suggests that *that* is indeed a lexical item.

The fact that complementizers are lexical items and exhibit meaning was recognized in Bresnan (1970) and discussed in great detail in Bresnan (1972). Bresnan offers a range of cogent arguments to show that complementizers are not the meaningless elements that transformationalists have assumed, beginning with Rosenbaum (1967). That complementizers must be lexical items is a consequence of the Spelling Prohibition, cf. Brame (1978a), although it must be noted that the Spelling Prohibition itself follows from the theory advocated here. It seems that the basic point should be emphasized again—words should not be abused. Each and every one of them must be provided a phonological representation together with a functional specification. None can be spelled out, deleted, or altered by processes such as transformations.

7. EXTRAPOSITION AND GAPPING AS ANAPHORA

It remains to discuss and refute several additional filters proposed within the framework of the theory under critique and to account for the deviance of the (b) examples provided in the previous section under (63)–(67), repeated below.

(76) a. *the fact John was here surprised me
      b. *it came as a surprise to me John was here
      c. *it is unlikely John is here
      d. *I pleaded with Bill he shouldn't hire her
      e. *John believes (that) Mary saw Sam, and Bill, Sue saw Harry

Of these examples (76d) is out for precisely the same reason as examples such as the following.

(77)   a. *She demanded he leave.
      b. *The law requires he have a permit.
      c. *I insist she return promptly.

As noted in the previous section, lexical items such as *demand, require*, and *insist* select S̄ arguments in lexical representations, not S arguments. Hence the examples listed in (77) are all functionally deviant and incomplete. Now *plead* is another of the verbs which does not select S (although it like many other verbs selects additional argument structure, e.g. NP, as in *John pleaded the case*).

We might expect that the remaining examples in (76) are also functionally deviant. In fact such an analysis is indeed what will be proposed here. A cursory sketch of the idea behind an account of (76a)–(76c) is the following. For adjuncts to lexical heads such as *the fact, the idea, the claim*, etc., which are not relative clauses, we might take the index of the complete S̄ argument and set it equal to the index of the lexical head. Thus, assume that *that John was here* is indexed by *p* and that *the fact* is indexed by *i*. Then it is assumed that *p* is set equal to *i*. The operation would constitute part and parcel of the operation of composing the S̄ and the lexical head. We could then provide a complete interpretation for *the fact that John was here*. However, an example such as (76a) would emerge as functionally deviant for failure to allow composition of *John was here* and the lexical head *the fact*. This follows from the fact that *John was here* is not S̄, whereas S̄, not S, is required for proper indexing to ensue.[2]

An analysis of (76b) and (76c) can be provided in the same spirit. Following Emonds (1970) we assume that the "extraposed" clause does not originate in the subject position. In fact, it could not since all transformations are proscribed in the proposed theory. Now, as an alternative to extraposition, or Emonds' intraposition, we may simply identify the index corresponding to the subject pronoun *it* with the adjunct S̄ clause! However this identification is allowed only in terms of S̄, never of S. It follows that examples such as (76b)–(76c) cannot be provided a single index and hence be interpreted as a single phrasal type. Although *it came as a surprise to me* and *John was here* can be interpreted individually, there is no way to link the two, since the latter is not interpreted as S̄, and hence cannot be identified with the variable index corresponding to *it*. Although *it is unlikely* and *John is here* can be interpreted individually, again they cannot be linked due to the fact that the latter is not $\bar{S}$, and hence cannot be identified with the index corresponding to *it*.

The suggested analysis has much in common with the original idea proposed in Emonds (1970), with the inverse analysis proposed in Brame (1976), and with the suggestions found in Jayaseelan (1979). Thus, Emonds assumed that the adjunct $\bar{S}$ was substituted for *it* providing they are coindexed. Within the framework offered here, there is no need for a rule of extraposition or intraposition. In the case of well-formed examples such as *it is obvious that John left*, the necessary link will be effected by a rule of anaphora identifying the index of *it* with that of *that John left*. In the case of *that John left is obvious*, no identification is necessary. This kind of analysis, incidentally, makes ad hoc constraints such as Ross' Bounding or Chomsky's Subjacency unnecessary, as will be shown in forthcoming work.

Thus, we are left with example (76e), which should also be incomplete under the assumptions of the proposed framework. Within the theory advocated here, Gapping can be viewed in a more interpretive spirit. In particular, we may assume that function terms such as V can be inserted by rule, to be followed by the interpretive procedures and, crucially, a rule of anaphora which associates the index of the left conjunct of the gapping structure with the interpreted gap. The surface analogue of Gapping might be tentatively formulated as follows.

(78) $\phi \rightarrow V \; / \; A_1 \underline{\quad} A_2$, where A is an argument term $\neq$ S

Now let us consider a simple example such as (79).

(79) John eats spinach and Mary, kale.

We can proceed to derive a complete interpretation for (79) as follows.

(80) $((V(NP^o))(NP^s))$ Con NP^x NP^x by Composition
    $((f(i))(j))$ g k 1 and indexing
    where f = *eats*, i = *spinach*, j = *John*, g = *and*, k = *Mary*, 1 = *kale*

(81) $((V(NP^o))(NP^s))$ Con NP^s V NP^o by (78) [and rule (35)]

(82) $((V(NP^o))(NP^o))$ Con $((V(NP^o))(NP^o))$ by further Composition
    $((f(i))(j))$ g $((V(1))(k))$ and indexing

(83) $((f(i))(j))$ g $((f(1))(k))$ by Anaphora

(84) $Con(S_1, S_2)$ by further composition
    $h(p, q)$ and indexing
    where p = *John eats spinach*, q = *Mary eats kale*, h = *and*

This analysis allows us to insert a verbal function between any two argument types with the exception of S. That other argument types are indeed relevant is indicated by the following examples.

(85) a. John ate in the kitchen and Bill, in the dining room. A_2 = PP
      b. John ate slowly and Bill, quickly. A_2 = Adv
      c. John wants to leave and Bill, to return. A_2 = $\overline{VP}$
      d. John said that Bill left and Bill, that Mary returned. A_2 = $\overline{S}$
      e. In the kitchen are two spoons and in the dining room, two knives. A_1 = PP
      f. That John failed is surprising and that Mary passed, incredible. A_1 = $\overline{S}$
      g. To err is human, to forgive, divine. A_1 = $\overline{VP}$
      h. John ate spinach and Bill, kale. A_1 = NP

It is interesting to speculate why S cannot be considered as A_2 in (78), which gives rise to the functional deviance of the Chomsky/Lasnik example (76e). Perhaps this indicates that S is not to be taken as an argument term after all. but rather a special kind of term, which we might call a proposition. (Complementizers could then be viewed as functions which convert propositions into arguments.) If we then adopted the function/argument notation of Brame (1978b, 1979), the conditions associated with (78) could be eliminated.

There are many interesting problems and puzzles associated with gapping structures. My desire here is not that of providing a careful analysis of the complete range of such examples, but rather that of suggesting that a plausible alternative exists within the proposed interpretive framework which can provide an account of the deviance of examples such as (76e).[3]

8. THE MISSING SUBJECT PROBLEM

Let us now turn to the following examples discussed by Chomsky and Lasnik.

(86) a. Who do you think __ saw Bill?
      b. *Who do you think that __ saw Bill?

Chomsky and Lasnik incorporate into their framework an analysis which is due to Perlmutter (1971), as reflected in the following statement.

(87) Perlmutter's Filter: Any sentence other than an Imperative in which there is an S that does not contain a subject in surface structure is ungrammatical.

According to Perlmutter, examples such as (86b) are ruled out by (87). The obvious question to ask is how Perlmutter keeps (87) from applying to rule out (86a) as well. His answer is this: "In order to account for these examples, we must assume that when *that* is deleted, the S-node above the embedded sentence is pruned away," [p. 112].

Chomsky and Lasnik follow the lead of Perlmutter's suggestion and posit a filter within the framework of their approach. This filter is recorded below.

(88)   *[that [$_{NP}$e]]

They note that (88) would lead to deviance in examples such as (89).

(89)   a. the man [that [[$_{NP}$e] saw Bill]
       b. a book t arrived [$_{\bar{S}}$ that [$_{NP}$ e] may interest you] (*t* the trace of $\bar{S}$)

As a consequence of such examples, they alter (88) as (90).

(90)   *[$_{\bar{S}}$ that [$_{NP}$e] ...], unless $\bar{S}$ or its trace is in the context: [$_{NP}$ NP __ ...]

They go on to suggest that (90) is part of universal grammar and that therefore it holds of all languages (where *that* is suitably replaced, e.g. by -WH).[4]

Now let us see how these examples can be treated within a framework such as that advocated in the preceding pages. As one might suspect, examples such as (86b) will not be provided a complete interpretation. They will emerge as functionally deviant. Thus, we must propose an interpretive rule which allows us to insert a subject argument in the case of examples such as (86a), but not in the case of (86b). In this way, as we shall see, examples such as (86a) will be provided a complete interpretation. The relevant rule is provided in (91).[5]

(91) ϕ → NP^s / V__VP

With this rule, it is possible to provide complete interpretations for examples such as (86a), but not for (86b). Thus, after composition, indexing, and application of (91), we derive the following partial interpretation.

(92) $(F^q(NP^x))((V(VP(NP^s)))(NP^s)$
      $(F^q(x))((f(g(NP^s)))(i))$
      where x = *who*, f = *think*, g = *saw Bill*, i = *you*

Notice that NP^s, supplied by rule (91) before the related composition of it with its associated VP, is unindexed. Now it, as well as the operator prefix F^q can be indexed if we apply the rule of Operator Binding proposed in Brame (1978). Thus, NP^s will be identified as *x* and F^q will receive some index *h*, yielding a complete interpretation. Since rule (91) does not apply to the partial interpretations related to example (86b), it follows that the various parts of such examples cannot be composed so as to allow appropriate indexing. It follows that such examples are functionally deviant. We do not therefore need to appeal to filters such as (90) which make subtle distinctions between traces and nothing.

Perlmutter noted that there are languages in which sentences analogous to (86b) are in fact grammatical, citing examples from Spanish such as the following.

(93) a. ¿Quien dijiste que __ salió temprano?
          *Who did you say that __ left early?
      b. ¿Qué dijiste que __ pasó?
          *What did you say that __ happened?

Unlike English, such examples in Spanish are well-formed. Perlmutter went on to correlate these facts with the fact that languages such as Spanish, in contrast to languages such as English and French, allow deletion of subject pronouns, as illustrated below.

(94) a. Salió temprano.
          *Left early.
      b. Pasó anoche.
          *Happened last night.

Perlmutter's correlation is paraphrased in (95).

(95) Perlmutter's Correlation: If a language does not allow deletion of subject pronouns, it will not allow sentences such as (93).

To put the correlation contrapositively, if examples such as (93) are grammatical in some language, then that language must allow deletion of subject pronouns.[6]

Chomsky and Lasnik accept this correlation and attempt to explain it in the following way. They make a distinction between [$_{NP}$ e], "a category with a null content" and "nothing", which is the "result of deletion" and claim that those languages which allow free deletion of pronouns also allow deletion of [$_{NP}$ e] as part of the same process. They say that "the rules of mental computation 'see' [$_{NP}$ e]" in terms of the filter (90), but that "this element is no longer 'visible'" when deleted. The alleged explanation therefore rests on a very subtle distinction between trace and nothing.

Now if it is true that there is a correlation here, we must ask how it could be expressed in interpretive theories such as that advocated here. In fact, the correlation can be expressed, assuming that it exists. Thus, in Brame (1978b) it was noted that it is no longer necessary to assume that languages such as Spanish incorporate rules deleting subject pronouns. Instead we posit an interpretive rule inserting NP^s in the subject position of such languages, whereupon the indexing of NP^s will be determined in part by discourse considerations (and person of the associated verb). Now it would be this rule which could be utilized to insert the NP^s argument in the Spanish examples provided in (93), whereupon, once again, Operator Binding could ensue to provide a complete interpretation. In this way, the correlation is expressed.

In conclusion, we see that filter (90) is unneeded within the proposed framework and we need not assume that traces in addition to subject pronouns are "deleted", a result which we would deduce in any case, given the Spelling Prohibition, cf. Brame (1978a).

9. FOR-FOR AND FOR-TO

Let us now turn to the following pair of filters proposed by Chomsky and Lasnik.

(96) *[for-for]

(97) *[for-to]

They posit filter (96) to account for examples such as the following.

(98) a. *We hoped for for John to win.
      b. What we hoped for was for John to win.

They assume that in (98b) the subject derives from "hope for + for clause" by Wh Movement. Hence filter (96) is invoked to account for (98a) when movement does not take place.

One ad hoc consequence of this analysis is the fact that the trace *t* purported to be left behind by movement rules plays no role in the account of these examples, whereas it does in others, for example in filter (90). Whether or not the trace has a residual effect then is simply coincidental within the Chomsky/Lasnik framework.

More to the point by way of criticism, however, is the fact that *hope for* does not select a *for*-complement, in spite of the Chomsky/Lasnik claim to the contrary. Thus, *hope for* selects an NP, cf. *John hoped for that result*, and the object of *hope for* in (98b) is not the *for*-clause, but rather *what*, which is in fact an NP. Now this NP's index will be identified as the index associated with *for John to win*. This identification should be effected by a rule of anaphora.

This kind of analysis immediately explains the following facts in addition to the facts listed in (98a) and (98b).

(99) a. What John thought about was that Bill left.
       b. *John thought about that Bill left.
(100) a. What John argued against was that Harry should be present.
       b. *John argued against that Harry should be present.

Here we see an obvious parallelism with the examples listed in (98). Clearly, filter (96) has nothing to say about these examples, however, indicating rather strongly that such an analysis misses the point. By contrast, the anaphora approach should express the generalization.

This discussion indicates that there should be no rules deleting prepositions, contrary to common practice within the transformational framework. Thus, contra Chomsky and Lasnik, examples such as (101a) do not derive from (101b) by deletion of a preposition *for*.

(101) a. We hoped for John to win.
       b. We hoped for for John to win.

Similarly, example (102a) does not derive from (102b), in spite of the existence of examples such as (102c).

(102) a. We want Bill to win.
       b. *We want for Bill to win.
       c. We want very much for Bill to win.

To my ear, (102b) is clearly deviant. Under the Chomsky/Lasnik analysis one might expect it to be grammatical, given their analysis of examples such as (98) and the fact that the following sentence is fine.

(103) What we want is for Bill to win.

Example (103) again shows that the object of *want* is *what*, an NP, which is identified with the index of *for Bill to win*. Thus, the difference between (102b) and (102c) must be expressed in the lexicon and reside in the fact that in (102c) *want* selects an adverb plus complement, whereas in (102b), there is a violation. In example (102a) *want* selects an NP followed by a VP complement. Chomsky and Lasnik pursue the faulty sentential analysis of such complements which has been shown to be incorrect, cf. Brame (1976, 1978a) and Bresnan (1978). Thus, Chomsky and Lasnik assume a structure resembling that of (104a) instead of the correct structure (104b).

(104) a. We want [Bill to win]
        b. We want [Bill] [to win]

Let us now turn to the filter provided in (97). This filter is designed to rule out examples such as the following.

(105) *We want for to win.

Chomsky and Lasnik claim that examples such as (105) can in fact arise since "NPs can appear freely in the subject position of the infinitival complement ..." But this claim is simply false, since $\overline{\text{VP}}$'s need not have subjects at all. Rather $\overline{\text{VP}}$ complements are lexically selected by many verbs, including *want*.

We have, in fact, an immediate lexically based explanation for the deviance of (105), namely, *for*, like *that*, does not select a $\overline{\text{VP}}$ argument. Thus, proper interpretation cannot ensue in the case of the surface string provided in (105). This, incidentally, allows us to provide a general lexical account of a range of examples, including the following.

(106) a. *John thought about to leave.
        b. *Bill argued against to buy chenille.
        c. *Harry thought about to own a Volvo.

Notice, once again, the parallelism between the deviant examples in (106) and example (105). This shows that *for*, like *about* and *against*, does not select $\overline{\text{VP}}$ complements, not that a filter such as (97) is operative. Chomsky and Lasnik lose sight of such lexical generalizations by forcing restrictions into the domain of filters.

We see, then, that we can dispense with (96) and (97), which far from solving problems of English syntax, lead to loss of linguistically significant generalizations.[7]

10. INFINITIVAL CONSTRUCTIONS

We are now left with only two filters. One of these is the following.

(107)   *[V adjunct NP], NP lexical

This filter is designed to account for examples such as the following.

(108)   *John believes sincerely Bill to be the best man.

Here Chomsky and Lasnik once again incorrectly take *Bill to be the best man* to be a single constituent, when in fact *Bill* should be taken as an NP complement and *to be the best man* as a separate $\overline{\text{VP}}$ argument, as noted in the previous section, cf. Brame (1976) and Bresnan (1978).

A second set of examples treated by (107) is provided below.

(109)   a. *I believe sincerely John.
        b. *I like very much John.

Now in fact examples such as (109a) and (109b) can be interpreted when there is sufficient pause between the adverb and the following constituent, as is often required in the case of complex NP's such as the following.

(110)   a. I believe sincêrely the girl who told me that she could drink
            more jenever than anyone else.
        b. I like very mûch the girl who saved the cat from the mouse.

In (110) the adverbs are provided a special intonation contour and are followed by short pauses. The resulting examples are interpretable.

Now it is interesting to note that a single pause associated with the adverb is not sufficient when two distinct arguments follow the adverb as shown below.

(111)   a. *I put quickly the car that everyone likes into the garage.
        b. *I called loudly the boy who you saw yesterday to dinner.

In fact, the only way that these examples can be interpreted is to provide a second pause associated with the final element of the first argument following the adverb. But this is precisely the situation that we encounter in connection with the NP VP constructions as illuminated below.

(112)   *John believes sincerely the boy who you saw yesterday to be the best man.

This example, like those in (111) which contain two distinct arguments, cannot be interpreted, unless, of course, as with (111a) and (111b), a second pause is associated with *yesterday*. This seems to indicate that NP $\overline{\text{VP}}$ constructions should indeed be viewed as two distinct arguments of the verb and not as a single S argument as in previous transformational work.

We might attempt to explain these data with the theory advocated here by taking adverbs such as *sincerely* to be lexical functions applying to true VP's or to S's, but not to arguments such as NP's and $\overline{\text{VP}}$'s. In examples such as (109a) and (109b), without appropriate pauses, the adverbs will be composed with the NP's so that proper indexing cannot proceed. It is necessary to have an appropriate intonation contour and pause available for the adverb to be sensitive to the VP or S. In other words, it is necessary to break the link between the adverb and the following constituent in order for the composition rules to be sensitive to this distinction. It appears that we can do without filter (107), which resembles the type of phenomenon discussed in Ross (1967).

We are now left with one remaining filter which has not been discussed.

(113)   *[$_\alpha$NP to VP], unless α is adjacent to and in the domain of [−N] or
        α = NP (where the feature [−N] holds of verbs and prepositions)

This filter is slightly revised after (107) is introduced but this alteration is not crucial for the discussion which will follow. Filter (113) is designed to account for the (b) examples of the following.

(114) a. his plan for Bill to win
       b. *his plan Bill to win
(115) a. It bothers me for Bill to win
       b. *It bothers me Bill to win
(116) a. It is illegal for Bill to take part
       b. *It is illegal Bill to take part
(117) a. I want very much for Bill to win
       b. *I want very much Bill to win
(118) a. There is someone at the door for you to play with
       b. *There is someone at the door you to play with

Now there is an obvious parallelism between many of these examples and examples which were discussed earlier. For example, notice the similarity between (63) and (114), repeated below as (119).

(119) a. the fact that John was here
           his plan for Bill to win
       b. *the fact John was here
           *his plan Bill to win

This obvious parallelism goes unexpressed within the Chomsky/Lasnik framework since *the fact John was here* is ruled out by one mechanism, filter (70) and *his plan Bill to win* is ruled out by a second, filter (113). Now earlier it was suggested that *the fact John was here* was out for failure to permit composition of its parts, *the fact* with *John was here*. Exactly the same now can be said with respect to *his plan* and *Bill to win*. Thus, there is no need for filter (113); the examples provided in (119b) are functionally deviant.

A similar parallelism is obvious when we compare examples such as (115) and (116) with the earlier (64) and (65), repeated below for clarity.

(120) a. It came as a surprise to me that John was here.
           It bothers me for Bill to win.
       b. *It came as a surprise to me John was here.
           *It bothers me Bill to win.
(121) a. It is unlikely that John is here.
           It is illegal for Bill to take part.
       b. *It is unlikely John is here.
           *It is illegal Bill to take part.

Once again Chomsky and Lasnik miss this parallelism by utilizing the two different filters to rule out the deviant examples. By contrast, within the proposed framework, it follows that (120b) and (121b) are out for the same reason; they are all functionally deviant. This deviance follows from the fact that the anaphora analogue of extraposition applies to identify the indices of arguments such as $\overline{S}$ (or $\overline{VP}$) with the subject *it*, but not S propositions or NP $\overline{VP}$ argument sequences!

There appears to be a parallelism also between the examples provided in (117) and those provided earlier in (66), repeated below.

(122) a. I pleaded with Bill that he shouldn't hire her.
           I want very much for Bill to win.
       b. *I pleaded with Bill he shouldn't hire her.
           *I want very much Bill to win.

As noted in section 6, *plead* must be lexically specified to take subjunctive $\overline{S}$ complements. Similarly, in (122) *want* must be lexically specified to select a *for*-complement, (NP) $\overline{VP}$ complement, or Adv *for*-complement, but not an Adv NP $\overline{VP}$ complement sequence. Thus, the solution to (122) turns on pure lexical considerations. Once again the examples listed in (122b) will emerge as functionally deviant for failure to allow composition which will permit appropriate indexing. In this way, we are able to express the parallelism. In contrast to this, however, the filtering approach advanced by Chomsky and Lasnik fails. A similar explanation holds for (118).

Before going on to show that filter (113) leads to additional loss of generalization, let us pause to take note, once again, of a fact which has been stressed several times already. It is relevant to note that the "unless …" clause associated with filter (113) is needed to permit the following type of example.

(123) John wants you to leave.

We see that Chomsky and Lasnik mistakenly take the NP $\overline{VP}$ complement to be an $\overline{S}$ complement. It is simply a coincidence that verbs are mentioned in (113), as [−N], when verbs are typically function terms which are specifically designated in the lexicon to select argument structure. Within the framework advocated here, however, this is no coincidence. Words such as *want* do select NP $\overline{VP}$ complements as one possible argument structure and therefore the ad hoc statement need not be proliferated to special filters. It is ad hoc in the appropriate sense, i.e. lexical.

It is now possible to proceed to demonstrate that filter (113) leads to additional loss of significant generalization. Consider in this connection the following examples.

(124) a. *It is unclear what John to do.
       b. *I told Bill what John to do.

Whereas these examples are ungrammatical, the following are fine.

(125) a. It is unclear what to do.
       b. I told Bill what to do.

According to Chomsky and Lasnik, examples such as (124) are out for failure to undergo an obligatory rule of control, whereas the examples listed in (125) have underlying PRO following *what* and must undergo the obligatory rule of control. This analysis is vague in several ways. First, just what precisely is this rule of control? Chomsky and Lasnik do not formulate it. And just how is (124a)–(124b) ruled out when this unstated rule fails to apply? These crucial questions are not addressed.

One can readily see, in spite of the inexplicit character of the suggested analysis, that a significant generalization is being missed. Certainly we should shoot for the goal of ruling out (124a) and (124b) by the same general means we employ to rule out examples such as (120b), (121b), etc. The parallelism can be clearly seen when we compare the relevant examples below.

(126) a. *It is unclear *what John to do*.
       b. *It bothers me *Bill to win*. [= (120b)]
          *It came as a surprise to me *John was here*. [= (120b)]
(127) a. It is unclear *what to do*.
       b. It bothers me *for Bill to win*. [= (120a)]
          It came as a surprise to me *that John was here*. [= (120a)]

I submit that (126a) should be ruled out on grounds similar to those used to rule out (126b) and that (127a) should be interpreted on grounds similar to those used to interpret (127b). Recall that (126b) were ruled out on the assumption that *Bill to win* cannot be identified with the index of *it* since *Bill to win* is not the appropriate *for*-complement. (It is not even a constituent.) Also *John was here* cannot be identified with the index of *it* since it is not the appropriate $\bar{S}$ argument. By contrast in (127b) we find the appropriate *for*-complement and *that*-S complements so that identification can ensue. Now to express the parallelism of the (126a) and (127a) examples with the others, we must assume that *what John to do* cannot be identified with *it* but that *what to do* can. This can be accomplished by providing the requisite functional structure in connection with *wh*-words such as *what*. For example, utilizing the general method of Brame (1978b), we can assign the following partial argument structure in the case of *what*.

(128)   what; NP^x, $(F^q$ (__))($\overline{VP}$) or ...

The three dots in (128) indicate that *what* must be assigned additional argument structure of the type indicated in Brame (1978b) for relative clauses, direct questions, etc. Now if we take $F^q(NP^x)(VP) \equiv \overline{S}$, we can account for the relevant examples in exactly the same way that we account for the other examples in (126) and (127). Thus, (126a) will emerge as functionally deviant just like (126b), whereas (127a) will receive a complete interpretation, just like (127b). Notice the close link between this solution and the lexicon. Just as *what* must be lexically specified to permit only a certain type of argument structure, so must function words such as *for* and *that* be specified to select only certain types of functional structure. For example, the preposition *for*, in its complementizer function, might be specified as follows.

(129)   for; P^c, (__(NP^p))(VP) or ...

Again, *for* has other functions, a range of prepositional functions other than just the complementizer function indicated by the superscript c, cf. Brame (1978b) for a discussion of some functions associated with prepositions. Again, we might assume $P^c(NP^p)(VP) \equiv \overline{S}$ and may go on to actually distinguish the various $\overline{S}$ argument types in terms of superscripts, a step which must be taken in any case. The point is that once this lexical treatment is provided, it is possible to treat extraposition phenomena as anaphora where $\overline{S}$ and $\overline{VP}$ argument indices are identified with the index of *it*. This yields a unified analysis of the obviously parallel structures discussed without recourse to ad hoc filters which are inherently incapable of expressing the generalization. Once again we see that the Chomsky/Lasnik analysis represents a move towards expressing idiosyncracies in terms of filters, when they should be expressed in terms of lexical structure. In this sense, the filter approach has very much in common with generative semantics where many idiosyncracies are transferred from the lexicon to the transformational component, often as exception features, etc. Surprisingly, then, we find a good deal of similarity between Chomsky/Lasnik filters and generative semantics.

11. CONCLUSION

It appears that there are ample grounds for disbelieving that filters provide any significant advance in our understanding of the syntax of English or natural language in general.[8] Indeed, it has been argued that each and every filter posited by Chomsky and Lasnik is unneeded when we view matters in a more interpretive light.

In a sense, one might say that Chomsky/Lasnik filters are special cases of incompleteness. After all, both say what is not a phrase in the language. It should be emphasized, however, that this comparison is to some extent an invidious one and that the analogy is perhaps too charitable. For one can see that filtering within the Chomsky/Lasnik framework is simply one kind of device which defines what constitutes a nonphrase in the language. In addition there are other considerations; for example, those phrases which are not generated by their phrase structure rules and which do not satisfy their lexical restrictions, etc. are not phrases in the language. However, functional deviance covers all cases within the theory advanced here. It is a general way of defining the complement of the language in question with respect to the concatenated vocabulary. We could just as well define completeness and then define incompleteness derivatively. The complete phrases are then those phrases which are recognized by the grammar. This definition is general and is not ad hoc in the sense of filters within the Chomsky/Lasnik framework. Completeness is directly linked to lexical structure by way of composition and indexing. Chomsky/Lasnik filters are not directly linked. They recapitulate other obvious lexical restrictions. Thus, the following two examples are out for different reasons within their framework.

(130)   a. *John pleaded Bill leave.
        b. *John slept Bill leave.

Example (130a) is out because *that* has been deleted, making (130a) susceptible to filter (70). Example (130b) is out because the lexical restrictions associated with *slept* are not satisfied, i.e. lexical insertion. But I claim that both are out for the same reason. Both are incomplete for failure to satisfy lexically based restrictions on the argument structure associated with *plead* in the one case and *slept* in the other. Chomsky/

Lasnik filters are inherently defective in that such generalizations go unexpressed. We have seen many additional examples in the foregoing pages.

As noted on several occasions, the postulation of filters represents a move away from the lexicon by way of stating idiosyncratic properties which should in fact be intimately bound up with the words themselves. How is it possible that such obvious idiosyncratic properties could be formulated in terms of ad hoc filters when they should in fact be related directly to lexical structure? It is no doubt the belief that transformations apply to more abstract underlying structure to yield surface strings that is responsible. Such transformations include Wh-Movement and deletion in COMP, rule (9). As we have seen, such rules give rise to insuperable difficulties and provide a basis for many missed generalizations. It seems therefore that we should forego transformations altogether and work directly off the surface. When we do so, the future looms much brighter. Many general properties begin to fall into place and many outstanding puzzles admit of realistic solutions.

NOTES

[1] This rule of anaphora, which can be taken to be a rule of bound anaphora, must make reference to specifiers since, as is well-known, determiners can have an effect on the grammaticality of the associated relative clause plus head. We must also distinguish *wh*-words from relative *that* as indicated by contrasts such as the following.

   (i) a. *I saw many boys who Bill saw.
        b. I saw many boys that Bill saw.
  (ii) a. *He likes the same people who you like. [Emonds (1976, p. 190)]
        b. He likes the same people that you like.
 (iii) a. *the people who there are [examples (iii) and (iv) from Ross]
        b. the people that there are
 (iv) a. the legs which Sue has [inalienable legs]
        b. the legs that Sue has [alienable or inalienable legs]

Additional relevant examples can be found in Carlson (1977).

Finally it should be noted that focus constructions such as the following must also involve a rule of anaphora linking the variable index of the *wh*-word or *that* with the post-copular NP, PP, or S.

   (v) a. It was John that Bill saw.
        b. It is Mary who Bill likes.
        c. It was in the garage that Harry put the car.
        d. It is simply that Harry is dishonest that Mary believes is true.

This analysis of clefts supersedes that proposed in Brame (1978b); however, Operator Binding must nevertheless apply to the associated complement of focus constructions; hence the examples cited there were quite relevant.

[2] Here too specifiers are relevant for the proper functioning of this instance of bound anaphora, since the following contrasts hold.

(i) a. the fact that John was here
   b. *a fact that John was here
(ii) a. the idea that Mary is rich
   b. *an idea that Mary is rich

[3] For a good survey of many of the problems associated with gapping, see Sag (1976), which draws on Lust (197?). See also Li (1979).

[4] Maling and Zaenen (1978) note that the Chomsky/Lasnik filter "seems to miss syntactic generalizations within English" in view of the fact that the 'unless' clause apparently recapitulates the relativization process. It might be worthwhile to distinguish once again binding and anaphora, as suggested in section 4. Thus, filter (90) apparently recapitulates part of the general anaphora process which links the relative pronoun to the lexical head in relative clauses, and thereby leads to a loss of generalization.

[5] Rule (91) is generalized in Brame (1979) to account for the following examples adduced in Bresnan (1977).

(i) It's in these villages that we all believe __ can be found the best examples of this cuisine.
(ii) *It's in these villages that we all believe that __ can be found the best examples of this cuisine.

Such examples immediately refute proposals such as Perlmutter's in terms of subject.

[6] Maling and Zaenen (1978) argue that Perlmutter's Correlation is not the correct one and offer an alternative.

[7] Chomsky and Lasnik draw on an alleged dialect of English to argue that filter (97) is dialect-specific. If their data are factual, it would be possible to provide an analysis within the framework proposed here. However, it is probably premature to jump to conclusions concerning the grammaticality of the two examples cited, which follow.

(i) Who did you say you were going to try for to go to the church social with you?
(ii) Who are you going to try for to go to the church social with you?

Chomsky and Lasnik cite these two examples as grammatical in Ozark English. Before anything can be granted, however, an analysis of Ozark English which draws on more than a handful of examples is certainly required. One has reason to be skeptical, for notice how involved and lengthy are these examples. Typically long and involved examples can often misdirect the mind of native speakers with respect to grammaticality judgments.

Chomsky and Lasnik also cite the following sentence as grammatical in Dutch.

(iii) Wie heb je geprobeerd om te verslaan?

However, the judgment seems to be wrong in this case. Speakers of Dutch who I have consulted say that (iii) sounds strange whem *om* is present. The speakers I have consulted are not linguists, but rather naive theoretically unbiased native speakers.

[8] Additional pertinent criticism of the Chomsky/Lasnik filters can be found in the interesting paper by Iwakura, cf. Iwakura (1979). Iwakura's criticism has not been repeated here; however, we agree in concluding that deletion of material from COMP leads to undesirable results. I differ from Iwakura in that unlike him, I have not chosen to provide new filters to account for the relevant range of data.

REFERENCES

1. Brame, M. K. (1976) *Conjectures and Refutations in Syntax and Semantics*. New York: Elsevier North-Holland.
2. Brame, M. K. (1977) Alternatives to the Tensed S and Specified Subject Conditions. *Linguistics and Philosophy* 1: 381–411.
3. Brame, M. K. (1978a) The Base Hypothesis and the Spelling Prohibition. *Linguistic Analysis* 4: 1–30.
4. Brame, M. K. (1978b) *Base Generated Syntax*. Seattle: Noit Amrofer.
5. Brame, M. K. (1978c) Discourse and Binding without Transformations. *Linguistic Analysis* 4: 365–404.
6. Brame, M. K. (1979) Realistic Grammar. Paper presented at the Conference on Current Approaches to Syntax. Milwaukee, Wisconsin: March 1979. In this volume.
7. Bresnan, J. (1970) On Complementizers: Toward a Syntactic Theory of Complement Types. *Foundations of Language* 6: 297–321.
8. Bresnan, J. (1972) Theory of Complementation in English Syntax. MIT doctoral dissertation.
9. Bresnan, J. (1977) Variables in the Theory of Transformations. In P. Culicover, et. al., eds., *Formal Syntax*. New York: Academic Press.
10. Bresnan, J. (1978) A Realistic Transformational Grammar. In M. Halle, et. al., eds. *Linguistic Theory and Psychological Reality*. Cambridge: MIT Press.
11. Carlson, G. (1977) Amount Relatives. *Language* 53: 520–542.
12. Chomsky, N. (1971) *Problems of Knowledge and Freedom*. New York: Pantheon.
13. Chomsky, N. (1973) Conditions on Transformations. Reprinted in *Essays on Form and Interpretation*. New York: Elsevier North-Holland.
14. Chomsky, N. (1977) On WH-Movement. In P. Culicover, et. al., eds. *Formal Syntax*. New York: Academic Press.
15. Chomsky, N. and H. Lasnik (1977) Filters and Control. *Linguistic Inquiry* 8: 425–504
16. Emonds, J. (1970) Root and Structure-Preserving Transformations. MIT doctoral dissertation.
17. Emonds, J. (1976) *A Transformational Approach to English Syntax*. New York: Academic Press.
18. Iwakura, K. (1979) On Surface Filters and Deletion Rules. *Linguistic Analysis* 5: 93–124.
19. Jayaseelan, K. (1979) On The Role of the Empty Node in the Structure-Preserving Hypothesis. *Linguistic Analysis* 5: 247–92.

20. Li, E. (1979) Verb Gapping. Univ. of Wa. M.A. Thesis.
21. Lust, B. (197?) On Gapping. MIT ms.
22. Mailing, J. and A. Zaenen (1978) The Nonuniversality of a Surface Filter. *Linguistic Inquiry* 9: 475–497.
23. Rosenbaum, P. (1967) *The Grammar of English Predicate Complement Constructions*. MIT Press.
24. Ross, J. R. (1967) Constraints on Variables in Syntax. MIT doctoral dissertation.
25. Sag, I. (1976) Deletion and Logical Form. MIT doctoral dissertation.

THE OPACITY CONDITION, THE NOMINATIVE
ISLAND CONDITION, AND THE MYTH OF CONTROL

Sensei, I love these examples, but control, is it really a myth?

> *John promised Mary his love, #her love.*
> *John promised Mary to shave himself, #herself.*
> *John promised Mary love.*
>
> *John impressed Mary with his love, #her love.*
> *John pressed Mary for #his love, her love.*
> *John impressed Mary with love.*
> *John pressed Mary for love.*

Yes, gakusei, but only in their sense, for they miss the significance.

1. Introduction
2. Two Linguistic Puzzles
3. The Nominative Island Condition and the Opacity Condition
4. A More Realistic Solution
5. Chomsky's Case Filter: Another Ad Hoc Principle
6. Extending the Data
7. The Myth of Control
   References

pp 111-148
pp 183-213

THE OPACITY CONDITION, THE NOMINATIVE ISLAND CONDITION, AND THE MYTH OF CONTROL*

1. INTRODUCTION

In what follows, I will assume familiarity with the lexically based approach to syntax advocated in [6], [7] and go on to compare it with trace theory with respect to Chomsky's most recent revision of his Specified Subject Condition and Propositional Island Constraint [= Tensed S Condition] as the Opacity Condition and the Nominative Island Condition respectively. It will be shown that the revised conditions, very much like the earlier ones, serve to describe rather than explain the relevant range of data investigated. In contrast to trace theory, it will be seen that the data truly follow from the lexically based theory without recourse to ad hoc theoretical elaboration of the type required within the framework of trace theory. This result provides support for the more lexically based view of grammar.

The plan of the essay is as follows. In section 2, several of Chomsky's "elementary properties of indirect questions" are reviewed and in section 3, we take a look at how these properties are described by the new conditions. Section 4 provides a more realistic solution to the puzzles unveiled in section 2 within the framework of the earlier references [6], [7]. A third puzzle is discussed in section 5, where it is noted that yet another ad hoc device is required within trace theory to handle it. By contrast, this puzzle is immediately resolved without prestidigitation within the proposed theory. It is shown that additional generalizations go unexpressed within the framework of trace theory, which are subsumed naturally within the lexically based theory. In section 6, the claims for independent motivation of the trace theoretic conditions are examined and found to be false. The extended data do not provide a plausible argument for trace theory. Finally, in section 7, two reasons are advanced for the failure of trace theory. These include a fondness for lexical abuse and a mythical view of control.

*This paper was presented at the University of Washington during the spring of 1979.

2. TWO LINGUISTIC PUZZLES

The following examples and associated structures are relevant to what Chomsky claims to be the "truly explanatory function" of his Opacity Condition and Nominative Island Condition.

(1) a.   ... [$_{\bar{S}}$ who [$_S$ NP visited t]]
        a'. It is unclear who Bill visited.
        a''. John asked who Bill visited.
  b.   ... [$_{\bar{S}}$ who [$_S$ t visited NP]]
        b'. It is unclear who visited Bill.
        b'' John asked Bill who visited Mary.
  c.   ... [$_{\bar{S}}$ who [$_S$ NP$_1$ to visit NP$_2$]]
        c'. It is unclear who to visit.
        c''. John asked Bill who to visit.

According to Chomsky, the complement phrases in the examples are analyzed as in the corresponding structural configurations, where t is the trace left behind by application of the alleged rule of *wh*-Movement and PRO is an abstract NP, realized as [$_{NP}$ e], e the identity element. It is to be noted that this approach follows tradition and incorporates the otiose S node in spite of the fact that there is considerable criticism of it in the literature, cf. [2], [4], [8].

Now Chomsky provides us with what he considers to be several of the fundamental properties of indirect questions. For example, the following direct quotes provide us with a source of puzzles which must be resolved within any explicit theory of grammar, apparently.

Puzzle #1

In case [1a] and [1b], NP $\neq$ PRO; that is construal is impossible. For example, we cannot have such sentences as "John asked Bill who visited," meaning that John asked Bill which person he, John, visited or which person visited him, John: even though *ask* assigns control by its subject (*John*, in this case), as we see from [1c'']. [11:p. 9]

Puzzle #2

In case [1c], NP$_2$ cannot be PRO with NP$_1$ = trace. Thus, "it is unclear who to visit" cannot mean that it is unclear who is to visit some unspecified person." [11:p. 9]

Let us now turn to Chomsky's solution for these puzzles in terms of his Opacity Condition and Nominative Island Condition.

3. THE NOMINATIVE ISLAND CONDITION
AND THE OPACITY CONDITION

Within Chomsky's framework, the two puzzles would be translated into the following structures with respect to the examples mentioned.

(2)   a. *John$_i$ asked Bill [$_{\bar{S}}$ who$_j$ [$_S$ PRO$_i$ visited t$_j$]]
      b. *John$_i$ asked Bill [$_{\bar{S}}$ who$_j$ [$_S$ t$_j$ visited PRO$_i$]]
(3)   *It is unclear [$_{\bar{S}}$ who$_i$ [$_S$ t$_i$ to visit PRO$_{arb}$]]

In these examples coindexing is assigned by an extremely general rule termed COINDEX. In the case of the structures provided in (1), COINDEX applies in the following way.

COINDEX: an arbitrary occurrence of PRO in the embedded structure of
‾‾‾‾‾‾‾‾‾‾‾(1) is coindexed with some NP in ... or assigned the index
          arb indicating arbitrary reference if there is no lexical NP in
          ...

Now Chomsky notes that COINDEX can be constrained by his conditions, SSC and PIC [= TSC]. Thus, PRO in both (2a) and (2b) could not be coindexed with *John* since it is contained within a tensed sentence in both cases. Moreover, it is assumed that assignment of *i* to PRO and *John* in (2b) would constitute a violation of SSC and that assignment of *arb* in (3) would violate SSC.

In [11] Chomsky proposes to revise PIC and SSC as the Nominative Island Condition and the Opacity Condition respectively. These conditions are provided below.

Nominative Island Condition [NIC]: A nominative anaphor in S cannot be free in $\bar{S}$ containing S.

Opacity Condition: If α is in the domain of the subject of β, β minimal, then α cannot be free in β, β = NP or $\bar{S}$.

According to Chomsky anaphors include PRO, trace, reciprocal pronouns, and reflexive pronouns. The theoretical terms *bound* and *free* are defined as follows.

We say that an anaphor α is *bound* in β if there is a category c-commanding it and coindexed with it in β; otherwise, α is *free* in β. [11:p. 13]

Now, NIC is designed to account for the deviance of examples such as (2a) where PRO$_i$ is nominative by virtue of a special rule: "the subject of a tensed-clause ... is assigned nominative case by a special rule, though the phonetic effects, in English, are seen only with pronouns'' [11:p. 16]. In (2a) we see that PRO is a nominative anaphor and free in $\bar{S}$ containing S. Hence, this case is ruled out by NIC.

Example (2b) is ruled out by OC since PRO is in the domain of the subject of $\beta = \bar{S}$ and is free in $\bar{S}$. The same goes for (3), where Chomsky takes PRO$_{arb}$ to be free in general.

We see, then, that Chomsky would account for Puzzle #1 and Puzzle #2 by invoking special conditions such as SSC and PIC, and, now, his new revisions of these conditions as NIC and OC.

Let us now show that such ad hoc conditions are unnecessary when we view matters in a more interpretive light which does not provide for abstract underlying representations of the kind adopted within trace theory and standard transformational grammar.

4. A MORE REALISTIC SOLUTION

It is assumed that the reader is familiar with the theory of syntax advocated in [6], [7]. Within such a theory, we work directly off the surface and attempt to provide a complete interpretation for the string in question. If a complete interpretation cannot be provided, the string is not a syntactic phrase in the language; it is, in the terminology adopted, functionally deviant.

Let us return to the crucial examples. Instead of (2) and (3), we will attempt to provide an interpretation for the following strings, since we are working directly off the surface.

(4)   a. John asked Bill who visited.

      b. John asked Bill who visited.

(5)   It is unclear who to visit.

Now we must show that it is not possible to obtain an interpretation analogous to (2a) in the case of (4a), to (2b) in the case of (4b), which happens to be identical to (4a) since we are working directly off the surface, and to (3) in the case of (5). Since we are working directly off the surface, we do not commence with abstract devices such as PRO and traces. The devices needed relate, rather, directly to the lexical representations or to general operations on functional structure, the latter including rules such as Operator Binding, cf. [5], [6], Anaphora, cf. [7], and a few others.

Now consider examples (4a) and (4b). In order to derive a complete interpretation for any string containing a tensed verb, that verb must have a subject argument to which the VP function applies. The relevant rule of composition effecting this interpretation is provided in [6], [7]. When subjects of tensed sentences are missing, we can attempt to interpret a subject by applying the following rule, which is a special case of a rule introduced in [6].

Subject Interpretation: $\phi \rightarrow A^{n[s]} / F^x\_\_F^{vp}$, where x = op, v

This rule allows for the interpretation of a subject argument $A^{n[s]}$ when preceded by an operator function or verbal function and followed by a specific type of function, the VP function, a tensed phrase, not an infinitive! Infinitives are arguments, not functions, and are represented as A^{vp}.

Let us now see how we can provide an interpretation for (4), concentrating on the complement string *who visited*. We apply the rules of composition and the indexing procedure of [6], [7] and derive the following partial interpretations.

(6) $F^q(A^{n[x]}):F^q(y)$ $F^{vp} \equiv F^v(A^{n[o]}):f(A^{n[o]})$

$\quad\quad | A^{n[x]}:y$ $\quad\quad | F^v:f$

$\quad\quad\quad |$ who $\quad\quad\quad |$ visited

We have chosen to interpret *visit* as a transitive verb, which yields $F^v(A^{n[o]})$ by the requisite rule of composition of [6] which selects functional structure on the basis of lexical specification, in part. We could just as well have picked the intransitive lexical functional structure in which case we would derive $F^{vp} : f$, a complete interpretation for the VP function. Here we still have an incomplete VP function and an incomplete question operator.

At this point interpretation cannot proceed further by application of rules of composition and indexing. However, the rule of Subject Interpretation can now apply to yield the following.

(7) $F^q(A^{n[x]}):F^q(y)$ $A^{n[s]}$ $F^{vp} = F^v(A^{n[o]}):f(A^{n[o]})$

$\quad\quad | A^{n[x]}:y$ $\quad\quad\quad | F^v:f$

$\quad\quad\quad |$ who $\quad\quad\quad |$ visited

Now the rules of composition and indexing procedure can operate to yield the following interpretation as the root of the composed structure.

(8) $(F^q(A^{n[x]}))((f(A^{n[o]}))(A^{n[s]}))$: $F^q(y)((f(A^{n[o]}))(A^{n[s]}))$
    where $y = who$, $f = visited$

To (8), a second rule operating on functional structure can apply, the rule of Operator Binding, cf. [5], [6]. This rule will bind the unspecified argument $A^{n[s]}$ or $A^{n[o]}$ to y, depending on whether we take x to be o or s. (It will also supply an index for the operator prefix F^q.) In either case, we are left with one uninterpreted argument, either $A^{n[s]}$ or $A^{n[o]}$. (We are assuming that *who* can be objective in the dialect under discussion; if not, then it could only be interpreted as subject, this difference being reflected in the actual lexical specification of *who*.) We see, then, that the phrase is not complete with respect to the attempted interpretation. This simply means that there is no analogue to the interpretations provided in (2a) and (2b) within Chomsky's framework. But we accomplish this result without recourse to special constraints such as NIC and OC.

Now consider the fact that an interpretation analogous to (3) is simply impossible within the framework of lexically based syntax advocated here. This follows from the fact that infinitive phrases are arguments, not functions. Consequently, the rule of Subject Interpretation cannot apply to supply a subject argument $A^{n[s]}$ when we attempt to interpret the following example.

(9) It is unclear who to visit.

We will derive a complete interpretation only when *who* is interpreted as $A^{n[o]}$, whereupon Operator Binding will identify the index y of *who* with the unspecified object argument of *visit*. A complete interpretation is derived by identification of the index of *it* with the index corresponding to *who to visit*. This identification is the interpretive analogue of extraposition, suggested in [7].

The theory advanced here is much more lexically based than trace theory. Thus, *who* will include the following functional structure in its lexical specification, among others.

(10) who; $A^{n[x]}$, $F^q((\_))(A^{vp})$

Abstract devices such as PRO are not part of underlying representations. The surface is mediated directly by lexical specifications together with general interpretive procedures such as those proposed in [6], [7].

5. CHOMSKY'S CASE FILTER: ANOTHER AD HOC PRINCIPLE

It would be of some interest if additional puzzles followed directly from the more interpretively based approach which did not follow from trace theory without further elaboration. In fact, this is precisely what we find to be the case, as will be shown in this section.

Chomsky provides us with yet another puzzle relating to indirect questions. It is summarized in the following direct quote.

Puzzle #3

In case [1c], NP_1 must be PRO; that is, control is obligatory. There is no such sentence as "it is unclear who Bill to visit" meaning that it is unclear which person Bill is to visit, nor can NP_2 be missing, even though *visit* can be intransitive. [11:p. 9]

The third puzzle, then, is to account for the ungrammaticality of the following examples, which are represented in terms of the following structures within trace theory.

(11)   a. *It is unclear [$_{\bar{s}}$ who$_i$ [$_s$ Bill to visit t$_i$]]
        b. *It is unclear [$_s$ who$_i$ [$_s$ t$_i$ to visit]]

Chomsky remarks that the "only property of indirect questions that does not fall under SSC and PIC [and hence NIC and OC, MKB] is the last one mentioned: the fact that control is obligatory in the case of an infinitive" [11:p. 9]. He summarizes his discussion, which I have included as puzzles #1, #2, and #3 as follows.

These are the elementary properties of indirect questions. They might be described in various ways ... In effect, the Specified Subject Condition (henceforth, SSC) and the Propositional Island Condition (henceforth, PIC; alternatively, the "Tensed-S condition") of the references cited imply most of these properties [but not the last, MKB]. To put it differently, some version of SSC and PIC is independently motivated by these properties of indirect questions, and is therefore available elsewhere in grammar to serve a truly explanatory function. [11:p. 9]

We have already seen that the properties expressed as Puzzle #1 and #2 can be explained without recourse to ad hoc conditions such as SSC and PIC, or NIC and OC. This shows, I believe, that the claim to a "truly explanatory function" is false. This demonstration carries all the more force in view of the fact that Puzzle #3, which is not covered by Chomsky's NIC and OC, is immediately explained without further elaboration within the interpretive theory which is more lexically based than trace theory. To see this, recall that we work directly off the surface. Hence, both (11a) and (11b) must be interpreted in terms of the following string.

(12)   It is unclear who Bill to visit.

Now there is simply no way to interpret (12) within the proposed theory. This follows from the fact that *who* does not select NP $\overline{\text{VP}}$ argument sequences. Although *who* may select a $\overline{\text{VP}}$ argument, as in the partial lexical specification provided in (10), there is no provision for both NP and $\overline{\text{VP}}$, as noted earlier in [7]. Thus, the heart of the explanation, once again, resides in the lexicon, not in ad hoc conditions.

Now the deviance of (12) truly follows without elaboration within the lexically based theory, whereas new ad hoc devices are required within trace theory. Thus, Chomsky introduces the following filter in conjunction with the case rules provided in (14).

(13)   Chomsky Case Filter: *N, where N has no Case.

(14)   Chomsky's Case Rules
       a. NP is oblique when governed by P and certain marked verbs
       b. NP is objective when governed by V
       c. NP is nominative when governed by Tense

It is claimed that example (12), *it is unclear who Bill to visit*, is ruled out because *Bill* is not assigned case by any of the case rules of (14). In other words, after the case rules apply, filter (13) marks the resulting structure as deviant since *Bill* has not been assigned case.

Clearly, such an analysis is artificial and contrived. It raises the discussion to an extremely abstract level where refutation seems impossible. Thus, it is clear, for example, that *he* exhibits case in English, as does *him*. The former is nominative, as opposed to *him*, which is objective (or oblique). Yet both of the following examples are ill-formed.

(15)   a. *It is unclear who he to visit.
       b. *It is unclear who him to visit.

Clearly, *he* and *him* in (15a) and (15b) exhibit case! Yet, Chomsky must now escape refutation by claiming that *he* and *him* derive from some more abstract representation and that this representation is not assigned case!

By contrast, within the theory which I have advocated, the integrity of lexical items is respected. Both *he* and *him* are lexical items and in neither case of (15) is a complete interpretation derived because *who* does not select NP $\overline{\text{VP}}$ argument sequences in the lexicon. It follows that the interpretive procedures will never apply so as to compose *who* and *he to visit* or *who* and *him to visit*. The Spelling Prohibition of [4] is satisfied and we need no case filter such as (13).

The ad hoc nature of the trace theoretical approach is revealed with even further clarity when we consider deviant strings such as the following.

(16)   a. *It is unclear who John hit Bill to visit.
       b. *It is unclear who among to visit.

These strings simply cannot be provided a complete interpretation within the lexically based theory since *who* does not select a sentence such as *John hit Bill* plus $\overline{\text{VP}}$, nor does *who* select a preposition such as *among* followed by $\overline{\text{VP}}$. This follows from the lexical specification provided in (10) in conjunction with the general interpretive procedures provided in [6], [7]. But, notice that (16a) and (16b) are out for the same reason as are (15a), (15b), and (12). In all cases, a complete interpretation cannot be derived as a result of the lexical specification associated with *who*. By contrast, trace theory must miss this generalization. Examples such as (15a), (15b) and (12) will be out because of one device, Chomsky's Case Filter, and examples such as (16a) and (16b) will be out for a different reason and accounted for by a second device, for example, phrase structure. This clearly misses the underlying generalization.

6. EXTENDING THE DATA

The following ad hoc devices are required within the framework of trace theory to describe the data of Puzzles #1, #2, and #3.

    i. A condition such as the Nominative Island Condition
   ii. A condition such as the Opacity Condition
  iii. A filter such as Chomsky's Case Filter

In contrast to trace theory, none of these devices is required within the lexically based theory advocated in [6], [7]. The careful reader should note, furthermore, that there is no counterpart to these ad hoc devices and filters which trace theory adopts. For example, in [7], it is shown that the effects of each and every one of the Chomsky/Lasnik filters proposed in [12] follow without elaboration from the lexically based theory. The relevant data discussed here and in the latter paper follow from the proposed theory without ad hoc elaboration and the reason is fairly simple. The cooccurrence phenomena that we are investigating are genuinely linked to lexical restrictions, one of the principal features of the proposed theory. Lexical restrictions are indeed localized in terms of lexical items themselves within the proposed theory, whereas they are elevated in terms of unnatural and contrived devices such as filters and conditions like NIC, OC, etc. within trace theory. When this latter approach is adopted with more and more distance placed between the lexicon and the surface strings, it follows, very much as with generative semantics, that new devices will be required, time and again, to force through the unnatural analysis.

Now let us pause for a moment to consider a wider range of data which Chomsky claims motivates his conditions. He claims that anaphors include such elements as reciprocal pronouns, reflexive pronouns, and traces and that conditions such as NIC and OC generalize to constructions incorporating these elements. Since this is so, he argues, NIC and OC represent genuine explanatory principles of grammar.

The fact of the matter, however, is that all the data discussed are explained within a lexically based theory without such conditions. Consider, for example, the following cases involving reciprocals and reflexives.

(17)   a. The boys$_i$ said that each other$_i$ would win.
     b. The boys$_i$ said that themselves$_i$ would win.
(18)   a. The boys$_i$ said that Sue hit each other$_i$.
     b. The boys$_i$ said that Sue hit themselves$_i$.

The examples provided in (17) are allegedly accounted for by NIC and the examples in (18), by OC. However, as has been noted elsewhere, cf. [3], a conditions approach to such data is misleading. It leads to a loss of generalization as shown by the following example.

(19)   The boys said that them would win.

In other words, *each other* and *themselves*, like *them*, is lexically specified as oblique arguments, written *ob*, which we may take to be a variable ranging over all cases other than *s*, the subjective or nominative case. Thus, *each other, themselves*, as well as *them*, will include at least this much functional information as part of their lexical specifications; this is indicated below in (20).

(20)   a. each other; $A^{n[ob]}$
       b. themselves; $A^{n[ob]}$
       c. them; $A^{n[ob]'}$

Of course, additional lexical information is required, such as number, anaphoricity, etc., but the point here is that all three example types in (17) and (19) are deviant in that a subject argument $A^{n[s]}$ is required for composition of the VP function with NP in accordance with the rules provided in [6], [7]. Such an NP would be the following.

(21)   they; $A^{n[s]}$

Composition could proceed if *they* replaced *each other, themselves*, or *them* in (17) and (19). We see, once again, that special conditions such as NIC and OC are not required to account for these data.

Let us now turn to (18a) and (18b). As noted quite explicitly in an earlier reference, [3], the rule of anaphora requires that reflexive and reciprocal pronouns be indexed with their subjects. (There is a special case such as *Mary talked to them about themselves*.) When this indexing takes place in (18a) and (18b), we have *each other* and *themselves* marked as anaphoric with *Sue* and this constitutes a violation of number agreement. This suggestion was put forward in [3], long before the appearance of "On Binding", yet we find no citation in the latter.

Let us now consider another type of example which allegedly motivates NIC, etc. Such an example involves traces and is provided below.

(22) $Mary_i$ seems that t_i likes beans.

Since movement of NPs such as *Mary* is completely free, (22) can be derived within trace theory. But such examples are purported to fall under NIC, since t_i is free in its associated $\overline{S}$. But, clearly, there is a gut-level response to this example which surfaces upon examination of the bare string.

(23)   *Mary seems that likes beans.

The problem is simply that (23) lacks an NP which could serve as a subject for complete interpretation of the string provided. Within the framework of lexically based syntax, then, (23) simply cannot be interpreted. This example, is similar in many respects to the example provided in (12). To see the parallelism, we repeat both examples below.

(24) a. It is unclear who—Bill to visit
      b. Mary seems that—likes beans.

In (24a), recall, *who* cannot be composed with what follows. Just so, now, in (24b), *that* cannot be composed with what follows. In both cases we cannot provide a complete interpretation because there are no provisions for composition. The lexical specifications of *who* and *that* do not include NP $\overline{\text{VP}}$ or VP as potential arguments.

We see, in fact, that there are numerous generalizations that go unexpressed within trace theory. For example, the following examples are all deviant for reasons completely analogous to the deviance of (23).

(25) a. *Mary knows that likes beans.
      b. *It seems that likes beans.
      c. *Mary insists that likes beans.

All of these examples are out for the same reason within the theory of lexically based syntax. By contrast, (23) is out because of NIC within trace theory, whereas (23a–c) are out because of different reasons, phrase structure or lexical insertion.

All of the data brought to bear in "On Binding" can be provided a completely natural lexical explanation provided we adopt a surface oriented approach. There is no independent motivation for conditions such as NIC and OC, contrary to the claims made on the basis of reflexives, reciprocals, traces, etc. Rather than belabor this point, let us now attempt to pinpoint the fundamental drawback of trace theory.

7. THE MYTH OF CONTROL

There are at least two keys to the failure of trace theory; one has already been touched upon above. On the one hand, trace theorists are forced to propose devices such as NIC, OC, filters, Subjacency, Recoverability of Deletion, etc. because of the unnatural remove they institute between lexical items and surface strings. They abuse lexical items by failing to recognize them as such, assuming abstract analyses, deriving *he* and *him* from some abstract source, never coming to grips with the surface data and never illustrating explicit derivations of the words in question. The actual phonetic detail is taken to be a trivial consequence of low-level processes which are uninteresting. Yet we see that such assumptions cannot be granted. We are not free to assume that the distinction between *he* and *him*, etc. is simply a trivial matter of detail. When we adhere to the Spelling Prohibition, such ad hoc analyses as proposed by trace theorists cannot be countenanced, cf. [4].

Besides lexical abuse, there is a second outstanding characteristic of trace theory which is largely responsible for its failure. This is the fact that trace theorists have been adamant in their reluctance to give up the abstract sentential source for infinitives, in spite of the fact that there is considerable evidence against the abstract source, cf. [2], [4], [8]. "On Binding" is perhaps the quintessential expression of this pernicious stance.

Now what is the reason for this continued bias against the obvious nonclausal source for infinitives? First, Chomsky assumes that puzzles such as those mentioned above follow naturally when sentential sources are adopted in conjunction with his conditions. But we have seen that such conditions and filters are in fact ad hoc devices that we can do without. Second, Chomsky assumes that a sentential source for infinitives yields a more general theory.

> Notice that this approach maximizes the uniformity of the lexicon and base system, just as in the case of the analogous indirect questions. It is clear that the base rules permit structures of the form V-$\bar{S}$ ("promise that ...") and V-NP-$\bar{S}$ ("promise Bill that ...," "persuade Bill that ..."). Verbs that take one or the other structure typically allow infinitives in place of $\bar{S}$ ("promise to ...," "promise Bill to ...," "persuade Bill to ...") ... We may therefore keep to what seems the simplest base theory: clauses can be finite or infinitive ... and there is no nonclausal source for infinitives. [11:p. 11]

The reasoning revealed in this quote is faulty in several respects. In the first place, it is simply not true that "verbs which take one or the other structure typically allow infinitives in place of $\bar{S}$." There are many verbs which select $\bar{S}$, for example, but do not "typically" allow infinitives.

(24) a. John demanded that Mary leave.
      b. *John demanded Mary to leave.
(25) a. John insisted that Mary leave.
      b. *John insisted Mary to leave.

(26) a. John thinks that Mary left.
      b. *John thinks Mary to leave.
(27) a. John denies that Mary left.
      b. *John denies Mary to leave.

Nor do verbs which select infinitives "typically" permit sentential complements, as illustrated below.

(28) a. John tried to leave.
      b. *John tried that he leave.
(29) a. John forced Mary to leave.
      b. *John forced Mary that she leave.
      c. *John forced that Mary leave.
(30) a. John telegrammed Mary to come.
      b. *John telegrammed Mary that she come.
      c. *John telegrammed that Mary come.

Citing two verbs which permit multiple complement types, such as *promise* and *persuade*, as Chomsky does, does not constitute an argument for an abstract sentential source of infinitive complements. Apparently, the following criticism is still apropos even today.

> Berman and Szamosi's reasoning is not new to the field. It goes something like this: Because some verbs take S complements, all complements to those verbs must be S complements. By parity of reasoning we could conclude that the NP direct object complement of *expect* in *John expected Mary* is really an S since we do find S complements to *expect*, as in *John expected that Mary would come*. Such reasoning, like that adopted by Berman and Szamosi, is obviously unacceptable. A real argument would necessarily show that NP patterns like S in a wide range of contexts or that postulation of S provides an explanation for otherwise puzzling phenomena. No such argument appears likely. [1:p. 198]

This criticism of several years past applies with equal force today to advocates of the position advanced in Chomsky's quote.

Next note that it is simply false that "this approach maximizes the uniformity of the lexicon and base system, just as in the case of the analogous indirect question." It is false because proscribing $\overline{VP}$ as complements to verbs gives rise to lexical gaps and gaps in phrase structure, as noted repeatedly, cf. [1], [2]. What "seems to be the simplest base

theory'' is simply an illusion, a hangover from initial work in transformational grammar.

Are there other reasons which underlie the widespread reluctance to
give up the traditional transformational analysis of infinitives as sentences? It seems that the notion of control plays a central role in this
controversy. Thus, commencing with early work on reflexivization, Lees
and Klima [13] proposed to restrict reflexivization to simplex sentences,
as illustrated below.

(31)   a.   John said that Mary shaved herself.
       b. *John said that Mary shaved himself.

Since reflexivization is apparently restricted to the embedded sentence in
(31), reason was found for positing an S in examples such as the following.

(32)   a.   John persuaded Mary to shave herself.
       b. *John persuaded Mary to shave himself.

Going hand in hand with this observation was the fact that subjects typically function as antecedent for the reflexive pronoun in simple sentences.

(33)   a.   John shaved himself.
       b. *John shaved herself.

Putting these facts together it was concluded, even as early as [9], that
infinitives derive from abstract sentential sources, with an abstract NP
subject.

The motivation for this leap to the sentential source is unjustified, however, as noted in [2], where a review of the arguments is provided. There
is another view which differs from the traditional transformational view.
The alternative view is that there is a relation which we might call *control*,
but that this relation need not be expressed in terms of abstract subjects,
whether PRO or otherwise.

The alternative view can be illustrated in terms of examples such as the
following.

(34)   a. John promised Mary to shave himself.
       b. John persuaded Mary to shave herself.

Let us agree that *John* controls *to shave himself*, the latter being a $\overline{VP}$

argument, an infinitive which does not derive from a sentential source. We might write this relation as follows.

(35)   control(John, to shave himself)

We agree to call the initial argument of the control relation the *controller* and the final argument the *controllee*. Now control is an interpreted relation and anaphora may be formulated in terms of the controller relation, making reference to the controller instead of the subject. Now clearly the lexical item in question plays a role in determining the controller relation. Thus, *John* does not control *to shave herself* in (34b).

The idea of deriving the controller relation as an interpreted relation is not simply a notational variant of the standard theory of transformational grammar or of trace theory. This follows from the fact that we may formulate the interpreted relation in a more general light. Thus, consider the following examples.

(36)   a. John promised Mary a shave.
       b. John promised Mary a ride to the store.

Here, once again, we can interpret a control relation, indicated as in (37).

(37)   a. control(John, a shave)
       b. control(John, a ride to the store)

Clearly, we do not wish to assume an abstract subject in the case of (36a) and (36b). To this Chomsky would agree, following some remarks he made on nominalization, cf. [10]. The point that is crucial for this discussion is that the interpreted relation in terms of obvious NPs in (37) can be taken to be the same controller relation that holds between NP and infinitive in the examples which are incorrectly analyzed by trace theorists. Infinitives qua arguments relate to their controller just as noun phrases relate to their controller. Thus, we encounter an analogous control relation in the following two examples.

(38)   a. John tried the pie.
       b. John tried to leave.

We interpret the following control relations.

(39) a. control(John, pie)
      b. control(John, to leave)

The fact that control need not be formulated in terms of abstract subjects—in fact it leads to a loss of generalization—shows that the standard account of control is a myth. Once this is realized, we can get on with the task of eliminating all transformations and proceed to develop realistic models of syntax which operate directly off the surface without ad hoc conditions and filters. This line of research, I conjecture, will occupy the attention of serious syntacticians in the coming years.

REFERENCES

1. Brame, M. K. (1975) On the Abstractness of Syntactic Structure: The VP-Controversy. *Linguistic Analysis* 1: 191–203.
2. Brame, M. K. (1976) *Conjectures and Refutations in Syntax and Semantics*. Elsevier North-Holland.
3. Brame, M. K. (1977) Alternatives to the Tensed S and Specified Subject Conditions. *Linguistics and Philosophy* 1: 381–411.
4. Brame, M. K. (1978) The Base Hypothesis and the Spelling Prohibition. *Linguistic Analysis* 4: 1–30.
5. Brame, M. K. (1978) *Base Generated Syntax*. Seattle: Noit Amrofer Publishing Co., P.O. Box 15176.
6. Brame, M. K. (1979) Realistic Grammar. Paper presented at the Conference on Current Approaches to Syntax. Milwaukee, Wisconsin. Published in *Essays Toward Realistic Syntax*, Noit Amrofer Publishing Co., P.O. Box 15176, Seattle.
7. Brame, M. K. (1979) Chomsky/Lasnik Filters Are Special Cases of Functional Deviance. Paper delivered at the Sloan Workshop at Stanford University in January 1979. Published in *Essays Toward Realistic Syntax*, Noit Amrofer Publishing Co., P.O. Box 15176, Seattle.
8. Bresnan, J. (1978) A Realistic Transformational Grammar. In M. Halle, et al., eds. *Linguistic Theory and Psychological Reality*. Cambridge: MIT Press.
9. Chomsky, N. (1955) *The Logical Structure of Linguistic Theory*. MIT Library.
10. Chomsky, N. (1970) Remarks on Nominalization. In *Readings in English Transformational Grammar*, R. A. Jacobs and P. S. Rosenbaum, eds. Waltham, Mass.: Ginn.

11. Chomsky, N. (1979) On Binding. Unpublished ms., MIT.
12. Chomsky, N. and H. Lasnik (1977) Filters and Control. *Linguistic Inquiry* 8: 425–504.
13. Lees, R. B. and E. Klima (1960) Rules for English Pronominalization. *Language* 39.

QUANTIFIERS, RECIPROCALS, AND RAISING

Sensei, is it true that Chomsky and Postal are both wrong?

Yes and no, gakusei. Chomsky is right to reject Raising and Postal is right in adopting an object structure. But Postal goes wrong when he adopts an underlying subject structure, and with it, Raising, while Chomsky is wrong to adopt the subject structure twice over.

1. Introduction
2. Controversy over *each other*
   2.1 Multiple Occurrences of Distributive Quantifiers
   2.2 Conjunction
   2.3 Distribution of *each other*
   2.4 Universal Movement Constraints
3. New Arguments Against the Transformationalist Hypothesis
4. *the men each* and *each of the men*
5. *expect NP VP* versus *expect S*
   References

QUANTIFIERS, RECIPROCALS, AND RAISING*

1. INTRODUCTION

There is currently a controversy over the status of sentences such as the following.

(1) a. John expected Mary to leave.
     b. John believes Mary to be rich.

Transformationalists seem to agree that the underlying representations of (1) contain an embedded S-complement as indicated in (2).

(2) a. John expected [Mary to leave]$_S$
     b. John believes [Mary to be rich]$_S$

However, they differ on the status of the appropriate surface representations. One group contends that there is a rule of Raising, which promotes the subject of the embedded sentence to the object position of the matrix sentence, yielding (3), after Pruning.

(3) a. John expected [Mary]$_{NP}$ [to leave]$_{VP}$
     b. John believes [Mary]$_{NP}$ [to be rich]$_{VP}$

A second group favors (2) as the surface representation of (1). This group denies the existence of Subject Raising.

Postal has argued for the existence of Raising in his extended study, [7], whereas Chomsky has argued for the nonexistence of Raising in [2]. In what follows, I will reconsider this question and draw the following conclusions: (i) the structures in (2) are not the appropriate surface repre-

*This paper was written during the spring of 1975 and is cited in my "Alternatives to the Tensed S and Specified Subject Conditions." It is published here for the first time.

131

sentations and (ii) the structures in (2) are not the appropriate base structures; (iii) hence, it follows that there is no rule of Subject Raising. Chomsky is right in denying the existence of Raising and Postal is right in denying (2) as the surface structures corresponding to (1). It follows that Chomsky is mistaken in assuming (2) to be the appropriate surface representations of (1) and Postal is mistaken in assuming Raising to exist.

In arriving at these conclusions, I will have occasion to review the arguments for transformationally deriving *each other*, a position adopted by Dougherty [3] and Chomsky [2]. It will be shown that this position is untenable and that *each other* should be considered a lexical pronoun, squaring with arguments provided independently by Fiengo and Lasnik [5]. It will also be argued that *each of the men* and *the men each* should not be related transformationally, contrary to the claims of both Dougherty [3] and Fiengo and Lasnik [5].

2. CONTROVERSY OVER EACH OTHER

Sentences such as the following have been the focus of several recent articles, cf. [4], [5].

(4) a. Each of the two candidates criticized the other.
     b. The two candidates each criticized the other.
     c. The two candidates criticized each other.

These sentences are, according to Dougherty [3], transformationally related. Thus, Dougherty derives (4b) from (4a) by a rule he calls Quantifier Postposition, and (4c) from (4b) by two rules he calls Quantifier Movement and *each other*-Transformation. To Dougherty's credit is the fact that he provides an explicit statement of his rules.

Chomsky [2] follows Dougherty in assuming a transformational relationship between (4b) and (4c). The latter derives from the former by a rule Chomsky calls *each*-Movement.

In contrast to Dougherty and Chomsky, Fiengo and Lasnik propose "that *each other* never arises from a transformation, but rather is generated freely as a deep structure pronominal NP" [5:447].

For the purposes of this discussion, let us call the Doughtery/Chomsky approach the transformationalist hypothesis and the Fiengo/Lasnik approach the lexicalist hypothesis. In this section I will review the stronger arguments for the transformationalist hypothesis and show that they in fact strongly support the lexicalist hypothesis. Additional arguments will

be provided against the transformationalist hypothesis during the course
of this evaluation. These will be seen to augment those already provided
by Fiengo and Lasnik [5] and thus serve to support the lexicalist
hypothesis.

2.1 *Multiple Occurrences of Distributive Quantifiers*

One alleged argument for the transformationalist hypothesis concerns
multiple occurrences of distributive quantifiers as illustrated in the (b) and
(c) examples that follow.

(5) a. The men talked to each other.
     b. *Each of the men talked to each other.
     c. *Both of the men talked to each other.

Under the transformationalist hypothesis, the deviance of (5b) and (5c)
follows since the *each* of *each other* originates with the antecedent and is
moved adjacent to *other* by transformations. Since both instances of *each*
in (5b) cannot be generated in the subject position, it follows that (5b) will
not be derived. Similarly, since both *both* and *each* cannot be generated in
the subject position, it follows that (5c) cannot arise. On the other
hand, (5a) does have an underlying source, namely, *each of the men
talked to the other*, and therefore can be derived.

This appears to be an argument for the transformationalist hypothesis
and Dougherty advances it as such. The evidence, however, strongly
supports the lexicalist hypothesis, as we shall see. In this regard, consider
the following examples.

(6) a. The men talked to one another.
     b. *Each of the men talked to one another.
     c. *Both of the men talked to one another.

Here there is no possibility of a transformational source for *one another*,
since *one* is not a distributive quantifier analogous to *each, both*, and *all*.
Yet there is a striking parallelism between the examples of (6) and those of
(5). Proponents of the transformational analysis must provide a nontransformational account of the deviance of (6b) and (6c). But this leads to
a loss of generalization since (6b) and (6c) are ruled out by one means, and
(5b) and (5c) are ruled out by a different means. Clearly, the nontransfor-

mational account of the deviance of (6b) and (6c) should extend to the examples provided in (5b) and (5c). This extension cuts the ground out from under the transformational argument.

It should also be noted that the presence of *each other* does not always preclude the appearance of a distributive quantifier with the antecedent, a fact which argues against the transformationalist hypothesis. Thus, the following example is not deviant, although one should expect it to be under the assumptions of the transformational hypothesis.

(7)   All of the men talked to each other.

Linguists as far apart in theoretical orientation as Postal on the one hand and Fiengo and Lasnik on the other agree on the status of such examples and cite the following.

(8)   a. All of the men will hit each other.   [5:110]
       b. All of them were hitting and biting each other.   [7:72]

Dougherty attempts to blunt the force of such examples by postulating two quantificational realizations of *all*: " ... the quantifiers of amount would include a quantifier *all* and the distributive quantifiers would include a quantifier *all*" [4:42]. The *all* of examples (8a) and (8b) are, according to this suggestion, quantifiers of amount, not distributive quantifiers. In this way, Dougherty attempts to dismiss the apparent counterexamples to the transformationalist hypothesis. The suggestion, however, appears to raise new questions, which may not have a satisfactory answer, indicating that we are actually dealing with a single quantifier type. Thus, the double source for *all* predicts ambiguities for examples such as *all of the men left*, where *all* in one case is an amount quantifier and in another is a distributive quantifier. Yet it is not clear that the relevant ambiguity can be perceived. True, such examples can mean that the men left together or separately, but this is a general property of examples without quantifiers, such as *the men left*, where we clearly do not wish to postulate a distinction.

Further evidence corroborating the incorrectness of the transformationalist hypothesis with respect to multiple occurrence of distributive quantifiers concerns the fact that there are examples which allow *both* to be associated with the antecedent of *each other*. Thus, the following example is quite natural.

(9)   Of the five boys, only John and Bill both shouted at each other
       simultaneously.

Such examples should not be possible, given the transformational approach.

We see, in conclusion, that multiple occurrences of distributive quantifiers do not provide evidence for the transformationalist hypothesis. Rather, we have found reasons to reject it.

2.2 Conjunction

As a second argument for the transformationalist hypothesis, Dougherty offers the following examples.

(10) a. John, Bill, and Tom each hate goats.
      a′ John, Bill, and Tom hated each other.
      b. *John, Bill, or Tom each hate goats.
      b′ *John, Bill, or Tom hated each other.

If *each other* derives according to the transformationalist hypothesis, it follows that when the distributive quantifier *each* permits a conjunction, as in (10a), there will be a corresponding grammatical sentence with *each other*, as in (10a′); when *each* disallows a particular conjunction, as in (10b), it also follows that the corresponding example with *each other* should be ungrammatical, as in (10b′). Since this distribution of data is actually observed in (10), it appears to constitute evidence favoring the transformationalist hypothesis.

Further investigation shows just the opposite. Relevant data include the following examples.

(11) a. John, Bill and Tom each criticized the officials.
      a′ John, Bill, and Tom criticized one another.
      b. *John, Bill, or Tom each criticized the officials.
      b′ *John, Bill, or Tom criticized one another.

These examples parallel those provided above in (10). In place of *each other*, the reciprocal pronoun *one another* has been substituted. Since *one* is not a distributive quantifier, it will not be moved into place by a transformation. Yet *one another* exhibits a similar distribution to *each other* in these examples. Advocates of the transformationalist hypothesis will need a separate device to rule out (11b′), while utilizing a transformational device to explain (10b′). This amounts to a loss of generalization. The same device should be used to rule out both examples, and this entails a nontransformational device in view of (11b′).

The deviance of these examples is not particularly mysterious. It appears that *each other* and *one another* are anaphoric pronouns which are plural in number. Yet disjunctions are singular, not plural. Thus, the judgments relating to the following examples with reflexive pronouns parallel those for the (a'), (b), and (b') examples in (10) and (11).

(12) a. John, Bill, and Tom hate themselves.
      b. *John, Bill, or Tom each hate themselves.
      c. *John, Bill, or Tom hated themselves.

Clearly there is a deeper generalization here that relates to number agreement, not to *each* per se. This, once again, shows that the transformational hypothesis is misguided.

2.3 *Distribution of* **each other**

As a third argument for the transformationalist hypothesis, Dougherty notes that "no ad hoc rules need be postulated ... to account for the correct distribution of the pronoun *each other*, since this is accounted for by independently motivated rules ..." [3:884]. Thus, the deviance of the following example follows from the transformational analysis.

(13) *Each other will win.

Since the *each* of *each other* moves from its antecedent and since there is no antecedent in (13) to provide a source for *each*, it follows that *each other* simply could not arise.

This approach, however, leads, once again, to a loss of generalization. The missed generalization becomes obvious when we consider examples such as the following.

(14) a. *One another will win.
      b. *Himself will win.
      c. *Him will win.

Advocates of the transformationalist hypothesis must rule out the examples in (14) by an independent nontransformational device, but surely this device should be utilized to rule out (13). To fail to do so is to miss a generalization. To do so, however, is to admit that examples such as (13) provide no evidence for the transformationalist hypothesis.

Again, these examples provide no mystery. All violate the requirement that subjects of tensed phrases must be subjective pronouns. If we take *each other, one another, himself*, and *him* all to be objective pronouns, then all violate this requirement.

Let us also note that the transformationalist hypothesis does not in fact predict the correct distribution of *each other*. Thus, Postal has noted that this approach predicts deviance for examples with two occurrences of *each other*, where there is only a single subject antecedent. Such examples include the following, (15a) being due to Postal [6:723].

(15) a. The men talked to each other about each other.
      b. Those two men saw each other and each other's wives.

Such examples cannot be generated under the transformationalist hypothesis and thus constitute evidence against it.

2.4 *Universal Movement Constraints*

Dougherty claims that "a fourth argument in support" of the transformationalist hypothesis "involves a putative language universal." This is Chomsky's Universal Movement Constraint which prohibits the introduction of "morphological material into a configuration dominated by S once the cycle of transformational rules has already completed its application to this configuration" [3:885]. This alleged constraint, argues Dougherty, accounts for the deviance of (16b).

(16) a. John, Bill, and Tom each thought that Mary had stopped seeing the others.
      b. *John, Bill, and Tom thought that Mary had stopped seeing each other.

According to Dougherty, Chomsky's constraint keeps *each* from moving into the embedded S in (16b) from its matrix position in (16a). This result follows, it is argued, only if *each other* derives from (16a) by a transformation. Chomsky [2], of course, adopts Dougherty's suggestion and revises his constraint as the Tensed S and Specified Subject Conditions.

In fact, the alleged constraint does not account for (16b), nor do the new conditions which Chomsky introduces, without loss of generalization. To see this, note that the transformational hypothesis does not subsume the following examples.

(17) a. *John, Bill, and Tom thought that Mary had stopped seeing one
          another.
      b. *John, Bill, and Tom thought that Mary had stopped seeing
          themselves.

What goes wrong with these examples is a violation of number concord
between anaphoric pronouns and the subject *Mary*. The pronouns *one
another* and *themselves* are plural, whereas *Mary* is singular. The same
goes for (16b), where *each other* is plural. If we formulate anaphora so as
to identify the anaphoric pronoun with its subject, then the generalization
can be expressed in terms of ultimate number concord violation. If we
attempt to account for (16b) by means of a transformation moving *each*,
we miss this generalization.

3. NEW ARGUMENTS AGAINST THE TRANSFORMATIONALIST HYPOTHESIS

We have seen that the evidence adduced in support of the transformationalist hypothesis actually favors the lexicalist hypothesis. Let us
now turn to additional facts bearing out this conclusion.
   The foregoing discussion indicates that *each other* is a lexical pronoun.
This conclusion is supported by Fiengo and Lasnik's observation relating
to particles. It is well known that in the stress-neutral case, particles may
not precede pronouns. Thus, (18a) is fine, while (18b) is decidedly ill-
formed when *up* is given the particle interpretation.

(18) a. John looked her up.
      b. *John looked up her.

This distinction does not exist in the case of nonpronominal NPs.

(19) a. John looked Mary up.
      b. John looked up Mary.

Now it is interesting that the pronominal distribution holds of *each other*,
as illustrated below, where *up* is again interpreted as a particle.

(20) a. The two boys looked each other up.
      b. *The two boys looked up each other.

Fiengo and Lasnik's observation shows that *each other* is a pronoun. It can now be extended to argue against the transformational hypothesis, since *the other* exhibits the nonpronominal NP distribution.

(21) a. The two boys each looked up the other.
      b. The two boys each looked the other up.

Clearly it is no coincidence that *the other* functions as a nonpronominal NP while *each other* functions as a pronoun. But this is sheer coincidence under the transformationalist hypothesis. How is it that the movement transformation just happens to convert the nonpronominal NP to a pronominal NP? By contrast, if *each other* is a lexical pronoun, then it is not a coincidence that it functions like *one another* and other lexical pronouns from which it not only follows that we find (21) above, but it also follows that we obtain the following distinction.

(22) a. The two men each thought that the other would win.
      b. *The two men thought that each other would win.

Example (22b) is deviant because *each other*, like other analogous anaphoric pronouns is objective, as noted earlier. By contrast, *the other* is not an objective pronoun and can function as subject. We thus find that (22b) is out for the same reason as the following.

(23) a. *The two men thought that one another would win.
      b. *The two men thought that themselves would win.

There are, in fact, plenty of examples showing that *each other* and *the other* must be distinguished.

(24) a. Each of the two clowns pretended to be funnier than the other.
      b. *The two clowns pretended to be funnier than each other.
(25) a. On successive days, each of the two boys is smarter than the other.
      b. *On successive days, the two boys are smarter than each other.

Perhaps it is wrong to star the (b) examples, but it is clear that a quite distinct reading is perceived, the (b) examples involving a contradictory reading.

There are, in fact, examples which are not treated by the alleged movement constraint, or its modern progeny.

(26) a. Each of the two girls left without the other.
      b. *The two girls left without each other.

Such examples show that *each other* does not exhibit a distribution coextensive with *the other*, a somewhat embarrassing state of affairs for the transformationalist hypothesis. Such examples show that *the other* may appear in environments in which *each other* turns out to be ill-formed, perhaps semantically. The following examples illustrate the converse.

(27) a. *The two politicians each told lies about Harry and the other.
      b. The two politicians told lies about Harry and each other.
(28) a. *In addition to the other, the two heroes each loved their wives.
      b. In addition to each other, the two heroes loved their wives.
(29) a. *Each of these two toads, with the exception of the other, can be said to love all other toads.
      b. These two toads, with the exception of each other, can be said to love all other toads.
(30) a. *It was the other that they each scolded.
      b. It was each other that they scolded.
(31) a. *Sockeye and Coho salmon each does not spawn with the other.
      b. Sockeye and Coho salmon do not spawn with each other.
(32) a. *Each kick the other!
      b. Kick each other!
(33) a. *Chained to the other though they (each) were, they (each) still escaped.
      b. Chained to each other though they were, they still escaped.
(34) a. *If you two each help the other, you'll manage better.
      b. If you two help each other, you'll manage better.
(35) a. *Remembering the other made them each forget their troubles.
      b. Remembering each other made them forget their troubles.
(36) a. *I asked which men had each stolen from the other.
      b. I asked which men had stolen from each other.
(37) a. *Who here will each know the other?
      b. Who here will know each other?

Such examples can easily be multiplied. They show that *each other* occupies many environments disallowing *each ... the other*. This distribution is unexpected under the transformationalist hypothesis.

The situation is even worse for proponents of the transformationalist hypothesis, for there are examples for which there is no plausible source for *each*!

(38) a. To challenge each other would lead to war.

      b. Challenging each other would ultimately amount to fighting each other.

      c. Imprisoned with each other for fifteen years, the two inmates each grew tired of the other.

Consider, for example, (38b). What is the source of the two instances of *each* under the transformationalist hypothesis? No acceptable answer appears likely other than the obvious conclusion that *each other* is what it is, a lexical pronoun, generated under the lexicalist hypothesis as such.

4. the men each *and* each of the men

Another argument might be advanced in support of the transformationalist hypothesis. This argument might have to do with synonymy and cooccurrence restrictions. Thus, it might be claimed that the following are synonymous.

(39) a. Each of the boys hit the other.

      b. The boys hit each other.

If (39b) derives from (39a), by transformation, then both might be expected to yield the same interpretation, since both derive from an identical source. Second, it might be noted that similar cooccurrence restrictions apply in many instances. Thus, when (39a) is grammatical, so is (39b). And when an underlying alleged source is ungrammatical, as in (40a) below, then so is the corresponding derived example in (40b).

(40) a. *Each of the man hit the other.

      b. *The man hit each other.

The cooccurrence argument fails, as noted in the previous section. But it does so even here in connection with examples such as (40). This follows from the fact that the following examples illustrate a parallelism with (40), but here there is no plausible analogous underlying source.

(41) a. *The man hit one another.

      b. *The man hit themselves.

Again, the transformationalist must lose a generalization, accounting for the deviance of (40b) by one mechanism and (41) by another. Clearly, (40b) should be ruled out by the same mechanism which rules out (41a) and (41b), which does not relate to distributive quantifiers per se. All involve a violation of number concord between the anaphoric pronoun and its antecedent; this shows that *each other*, like *one another* and *themselves*, is an anaphoric pronoun. There is no need to derive *each other* from a more abstract source.

Dougherty makes an observation which is related to this discussion. Thus, he cites the following examples.

(42) a. Each of the men will drink a beer.
      b. The men each will drink a beer.

Dougherty claims that Quantifier Postposition "accounts for two facts, the (a) and (b) sentences are synonymous" and "the quantifier in the (a) sentence has the same selection restrictions as the quantifier in the (b) sentence" [3:877], although he qualifies this comment, noting that "synonymy and identity of selection restrictions are not motivation enough to establish a transformational relation" [3:877].

Now let us examine Dougherty's comments more carefully. His claim is clearly that synonymy and selection restrictions are preserved under transformation and that the results in (42) are consistent with this claim. He indicates that the alleged transformation of Quantifier Postposition "accounts" for such "facts". But if synonymy and selection restrictions are preserved under Quantifier Postposition, they should also be preserved under the transformations which are alleged to give rise to *each other*. Therefore, the transformational hypothesis would seem to predict that the following are synonymous.

(43) a. Each of the two men slaughtered the other.
      b. The two men slaughtered each other.

These examples are not synonymous. Two men can slaughter each other by striking each other simultaneously with an ax, but (43a) would not be appropriate in this case; rather (43b) would be used. On the other hand, it would not be peculiar to say that each of the two men slaughtered the other in successive games of chess, though in this sense (43b) would be peculiar and inappropriate if the slaughtering occurred on the part of Sam in the first game and on the part of Harry in the second. We see, then, that the subject-predicate relation differs for (43a) and (43b) and that this difference can be crucial. Thus, (43a) and (43b) are not synonymous, a fact recognized by Fiengo and Lasnik [5].

We see, then, that synonymy and cooccurrence cannot be summoned as an argument for the transformationalist hypothesis, in particular, for a transformational derivation of *each other*. Can they, however, be advanced as an argument for Quantifier Postposition, which is alleged to relate *each of the men* and *the men each*. It is interesting to note that Fiengo and Lasnik accept this relation as a transformational relation, although, as noted, they reject the transformation(s) deriving *each other*. I would like to suggest, however, that *each of the men* and *the men each* are not transformationally derived, contrary to Fiengo, Lasnik, and Dougherty. Crucial examples include the following.

(44) a. There are two boys each helping the other.
  b. *There are each of two boys helping the other.
(45) a. There are two squirrels both eating peanuts.
  b. *There are both of two squirrels eating peanuts.
(46) a. There are six thousand girls all singing. $\neq$
  b. *There are all of six thousand girls singing.

Now it has been argued elsewhere that there is no *there*-Insertion transformation, cf. [7], [1]. Rather, *there* should be base generated. And yet we find that the (a) examples are grammatical. If the distributive quantifiers *each, both*, and *all* derive from the subject position, then the (b) examples should emerge as well-formed. This is not the case, indicating that the relevant examples are not in fact transformationally related.

5. expect NP VP *versus* expect S

We have concluded that *each other* is a lexical pronoun and that it should not be derived transformationally. It has also been suggested that there is no transformational rule giving rise to *the men each* from *each of the men*. We can now utilize this result to argue against the abstract S structure which Chomsky posits as the surface structure of examples such as *John believes Harry to be stupid* and *John expected Harry to leave*. His proposal for surface structures is provided below.

(47) a. John believes [Harry to be stupid]$_S$
  b. John expected [Harry to leave]$_S$

The usual assumption is that the following are the appropriate surface structures, derived from (47) by a rule of Raising (and Pruning).

(48) a. John believes [Harry]$_{NP}$ [to be stupid]$_{VP}$
      b. John expected [Harry]$_{NP}$ [to leave]$_{VP}$

Let us refer to the structures in (47) as subject structures and those in (48) as the object structures. That the object structures should in fact be the base structures was argued in [1]. We therefore have three positions: the traditional position, accepted by Postal, that (47) represents the base structures and (48) the surface structures; Chomsky's position, that (47) represents both the base and surface structures; and my own, that (48) represents both the base and surface structures.

Now *each other* cannot occupy the subject position in clear instances of subjects, as noted earlier, cf. (13).

(49) a. *Each other are stupid.
      b. *Each other leave.

Hence, we should conclude that *each other* is simply not the subject in examples such as *The boys believed each other to be stupid* and *The girls expected each other to leave*. The evidence, therefore, points to (48) as the correct surface structures, as argued independently and at great length by Postal [7].

Since Chomsky takes the subject structures to be the appropriate surface structures, we might pause to consider his reasons for doing so. In [2], he provides three arguments for this position. Let us consider them in turn. His first argument is recorded verbatim.

> ... consider *The men were told to expect John to kill the other(s)*. If *John* is raised on an internal cycle, it will no longer be a subject when the matrix cycle is reached so that *each*-movement should apply to give *The men were told to expect John to kill each other*. Similarly, we have *We were told to expect John to kill me* but not *We were told to expect to kill me*, the former inconsistent with subject raising ...   [2:254, n. 33]

This argument is predicated on the existence of the Specified Subject Condition, introduced in [2]. Chomsky assumes that *each* cannot be moved past a specified subject, in accordance with this constraint, which is a revised version of the alleged universal constraint discussed earlier.

Chomsky's argument here is that if *John* is raised into object position (or originates there as I claim), then we would expect **The men were told to expect John to kill each other* since the Specified Subject Condition would not then be applicable. Since the result is ungrammatical, it follows, argues Chomsky, that *John* is the subject dominated by S.

This argument goes wrong in several ways. First, it has been shown above that there is no rule of *each*-movement. Second, suppose that there is a relevant notion of subject. It does not follow that subject need be defined as that NP directly dominated by S. In fact, we could take *John* to be a subject in the relevant example and still adopt the obvious object structure. Third, there is really no evidence for the Specified Subject Condition as formulated in [2].

What then is the reason for the deviance of **The men were told to expect John to kill each other*. Following Emonds' suggestion, cf. [1], let us assume that *each other* must be marked anaphoric with some NP which stands in some grammatical relation to the verb to which the anaphoric pronoun itself relates. If *John* is taken to be the subject of *kill* in an extended sense of subject, not the traditional *Aspects* definition, then *each other* will be marked as anaphoric with *John*. But here, as with previous examples discussed earlier, we end up with a violation of number agreement. The pronoun is plural, while *John* is singular.

The example involving disjoint reference can be treated in an analogous way. Two NPs must stand in a grammatical relation to the same verb in order to qualify for disjoint reference. In *We were told to expect John to kill me*, *John* and *me* are disjoint in the intended sense and in **We were told to expect to kill me*, *we* and *me* are marked as disjoint, which provides a violation of what is already stipulated about first person pronouns, namely that first person pronouns intersect in reference.

Let us now turn to Chomsky's second argument for the subject structures. Again, a direct quote, follows.

> Another problem is suggested by some observations of John Kimball, who points out that from *It was easy for Jones to force Smith to recover* we can derive *Smith was easy for Jones to force to recover*, but from *It was easy for Jones to expect Smith to recover*, we cannot form **Smith was easy for Jones to expect to recover*. Assuming subject raising [or underlying object structure, MKB], the two sentences are identical at the point where *it*-Replacement takes place. If there is no subject raising, the rule of *it*-Replacement can make the required distinction by permitting the NP moved to be followed by S (as in *Bill is easy to persuade that the moon is made of green cheese*). [254:n. 33]

The data mentioned in this quote should, I believe, be attributed to Kisseberth, who mentioned them in unpublished work around '67. We can see quite clearly that Chomsky's account does not argue for the distinction. Thus, it does not appear to be true that there must be an S following an NP for *it*-Replacement to be applicable. For example, in the case of *it is easy to please John*, there is no following S, and yet we derive *John is easy to please*, assuming that *it*-Replacement exists (which I do not, cf. [1]). Thus, Chomsky's proposal does not work. Second, even when a following S is assumed to exist with Chomsky's framework, we sometimes end up with examples which appear to be equally deviant as the *expect* example. Thus, consider the following parallelism.

(50) a. *Mary is easy to expect to participate.
      b. *Mary is easy to promise to be allowed to participate.

Although *it is easy to promise Mary to be allowed to participate* is fine, (50b) seems to be strange, certainly as strange as (50a). In fact, we seem to be dealing here with special properties of the predicates themselves, for notice the following data.

(51) a. It is easy to promise Mary (but not to deliver on the promise).
      b. It is easy to expect Mary (but not to see her show up).
(52) a. *Mary is easy to promise.
      b. *Mary is easy to expect.

These observations show that Chomsky's suggestion has nothing to do with what is in fact going on here. Thus, we find the following correlation.

(53) a. It is easy to persuade Mary.
      b. Mary is easy to persuade.

When the example without the extra VP complement is grammatical, as in (53), then apparently the same example is fine with a VP-complement. When it is deviant, as in (52), then the corresponding example with VP-complement is also deviant, as in (50). This correlation shows that Chomsky's suggested solution is not sufficiently general.

Finally, Chomsky offers a third argument for the abstract subject structure with abstract S. This argument relates to the following example.

(54) *Who do you expect stories about to terrify John.

The argument runs as follows, where the number reference has been altered to agree with (54) above.

> If there were such a rule [Raising], *wh*-Movement should apply, giving [54], analogous to *Who did you see pictures of last night, Who did you tell stories about at the campfire.* These forms, though hardly elegant, seem to me much more acceptable than [54], as we would expect on the assumption that there is no rule of subject raising to object position.   [250:n. 31]

Here the argument once again turns on the alleged Specified Subject Condition. Movement of the *wh*-word to yield (54) involves a violation of the putative condition, provided, the argument goes, *stories about who* is taken to be the specified subject dominated by S. This argument collapses when we once again observe that we are actually dealing with a more general phenomenon. Consider the following examples.

(55)   a.   John sent stories about someone to Mary.
     b.   *Who did John send stories about to Mary?
(56)   a.   John told stories about someone to his best friend.
     b.   *Who did John tell stories about to his best friend.

Clearly, these examples are relevant to this discussion. The (b) examples show that there is a deeper generalization to be expressed which does not relate to the notion subject.

We see, then, that none of Chomsky's arguments holds up upon scrutiny. There is simply no evidence that the subject structures should be favored as surface structures, nor is there evidence that the object structures should not be taken to be the appropriate surface structures. In fact, Postal has provided a wealth of evidence to support the claim that the object structures are the appropriate surface structures, cf. [7].

It is appropriate to ask whether there is any evidence that the subject structures are the appropriate base structures, or, alternatively, whether there is any evidence that the object structures are not the appropriate base structures. In [1] it has been argued that the object structures are in fact the appropriate base structures. The traditional arguments simply do not hold up. Thus, all of the following can be taken to be the appropriate base structures, as well as surface structures.

(57)   a.   John expected [Mary]$_{NP}$ [to leave]$_{VP}$
     b.   John believes [Mary]$_{NP}$ [to be rich]$_{VP}$
     c.   John persuaded [Mary]$_{NP}$ [to leave]$_{VP}$
     d.   John promised [Mary]$_{NP}$ [to leave]$_{VP}$

This conclusion in turn has important consequences for transformational grammar, as shown in [1]. A number of classical transformations must be abandoned and replaced by other devices.

We thus arrive at a position which is in a sense intermediate between that of Postal on the one hand and Chomsky on the other. With Chomsky we agree that there is no rule of Subject Raising, a rule which Postal accepts, and with Postal we agree that object structures are the appropriate surface structures, which Chomsky denies; at the same time, we disagree with both Chomsky and Postal in accepting subject structures, whether in deep structure, as with both Chomsky and Postal, or in surface structure, as with Chomsky. The claim that object structures are appropriate both as surface and base structures is a position which has far-reaching consequences for the theory of grammar, consequences which are, however, highly desirable.

REFERENCES

1. Brame, M. K. (1976) *Conjectures and Refutations in Syntax and Semantics*. New York: Elsevier North-Holland.
2. Chomsky, N. (1973) Conditions on Transformations. In *A Festschrift for Morris Halle*, S. R. Anderson and P. Kiparsky, eds. New York: Holt, Rinehart, and Winston.
3. Dougherty, R. C. (1970) A Grammar of Coordinate Conjunction, Part I. *Language* 46: 850–98.
4. Dougherty, R. C. (1974) The Syntax and Semantics of *each other* Constructions. *Foundations of Language* 12: 1–47.
5. Fiengo, R. and H. Lasnik (1973) The Logical Structure of Reciprocal Sentences in English. *Foundations of Language* 9: 447–468.
6. Jenkins, L. (1972) *Modality in English Syntax*. Doctoral dissertation, MIT. Distributed by Indiana University Linguistics Club.
7. Postal, P. M. (1974) *On Raising: One Rule of English Grammar and Its Theoretical Implications*. Cambridge: MIT Press.

THE BASE HYPOTHESIS AND THE SPELLING PROHIBITION

Sensei, the Spelling Prohibition goes far in spite of its simplicity.

Yes, gakusei, it even has implications for phonology, but it is for us alone. Those who abuse our friends, the words, cannot open their minds, for they know too much.

Introductory Remarks
1. The Base Hypothesis
2. Affix-Hopping and *there*-Insertion
3. Extraposition and Sentential Subjects
4. The Spelling Prohibition
5. Lexicalism vs. The Inverse Cycle
References

The Base Hypothesis and the Spelling Prohibition*

In the first section of this essay several arguments are recapitulated which appeared in an earlier publication [2]. These arguments turn on the nonexistence of Equi, a rule which has been posited by transformationalists working within the framework of the standard theory. The consequences of abandoning Equi are also reviewed and shown to culminate in what is called the "base hypothesis."

Section 2 is given over to new motivation for the base hypothesis. The basic argument concerns Affix-Hopping and existentials employing the expletive *there*. It is argued that a basic generalization can be expressed if Affix-Hopping and *there*-Insertion are supplanted with base generated structures. It is also suggested that VP gaps be generated directly by base rules. These results lead once again to the conclusions drawn in the first section. Thus, section 2 can be viewed as additional support for the base hypothesis.

Section 3 undertakes a brief reanalysis of sentential subjects and related phenomena. It is shown that a wide range of data previously described by constraints such as Ross's Sentential Subject Constraint and Island Internal S Constraint, Emonds' prohibition against multiple application of root transformations, Horn's NP Constraint and global Pruning, etc., can in fact be explained by a straightforward elaboration of the base. It is therefore suggested that Extraposition is not a transformation in the classical sense, a result consistent with the base hypothesis.

In section 4 a general constraint on the functioning of transformations is advanced. The effect of this constraint, called the Spelling Prohibition, is to choose grammars consistent with the arguments advanced in the first three sections. Thus, the Spelling Prohibition requires that grammars be formulated so as to be consistent with the informal base hypothesis sketched out in section 1.

The question of alternatives to the standard theory, including the

* This paper was delivered at the Eighth Annual Colloquium on Directions in Linguistics held at the University of Calgary on March 21, 1977.

inverse cycle approach introduced in [2] and Bresnan's lexicalist model, is touched on in section 5. Some evidence is introduced in this section to empirically distinguish the two approaches vis-à-vis the question of passives.

Finally, section 6 is an all too brief excursus into the transformational component. In this section a powerful constraint on the form of transformations is conjectured and alternative models are mentioned, including a hybrid of the lexicalist model and that introduced in [2].

1. THE BASE HYPOTHESIS

Within the standard theory of transformational grammar, a problem of overgeneration emerges. This problem has not really been confronted. It concerns the following examples:

(1) a. John tried to avoid the issue.
    b. *John tried for Mary to avoid the issue.

(2) a. I will persuade you to recognize the superiority of an Elna.
    b. *I will persuade you for John to recognize the superiority of an Elna.

(3) a. Mary wants us to provide genever for everyone.
    b. *Mary wants us for Harry to provide genever for everyone.

The problem is to avoid generating examples such as (1b), (2b), and (3b), while allowing for (1a), (2a), and (3a). Various constraints have been proposed to accomplish this, but none of these constraints touches the heart of the problem. They simply amount to redescriptions of the basic problem.[1] Rather than proposing new constraints which serve no independent purpose, we might alternatively question some of the basic assumptions which contribute to the generation of the ill-formed examples. Thus, taking (1) as a representative example, we might ask why (1b) should arise in the first place as a problem for the standard theory. The answer in this case is quite obvious. Example (1b) arises because (1a) is derived from an underlying structure incorporating a sentential complement, as illustrated in (4).

---

[1] To take just one example, consider Lakoff's absolute exception mechanism advocated in [28]. Lakoff marks predicates such as *try* with ad hoc absolute exception features so that they will obligatorily meet the structural description of Equi. In other words, *try* is syntactically irregular within Lakoff's framework for appearing in the structures in which it appears. For summary and criticism of proposals for dealing with examples such as (1b), (2b), and (3b), see Brame [2: 94–97, 103–107].

(4) a. John tried [$_S$ for John [$_{VP}$ to avoid the issue]$_{VP}$]$_S$

   b. John tried [$_S$ for PRO [$_{VP}$ to avoid the issue]$_{VP}$]$_S$

Whether one adopts (4a), as in the standard theory, or (4b), as in the extended standard theory, the very fact that *try* can be lexically subcategorized so as to select an S-complement gives rise to new problems connected with ill-formed sentences such as (1b), and likewise for (2) and (3) with *persuade* and *want*. However, if one rejects this basic assumption and adopts instead what is recognized to exist on the surface, i.e., a VP-complement as the underlying subcategorization associated with *try*, then the question of the ungrammaticality of (1b) does not even arise. Likewise, if *persuade, want,* etc., are subcategorized so as to select NP VP-complements in the case of (2a) and (3a), then the question of the ungrammaticality of (2b) and (3b) does not even arise. Rather, (2b) and (3b) are out for precisely the same reason as the following examples are out.

(5) a. *I saw Mary for John to leave.
   b. *Mary pinched me for Harry to speak up.
   c. *They all recognized Bill for us to forget our grudge.

Thus, *persuade* and *want*, like *see, pinch,* and *recognize,* do not select NP S-complements, although the former do select NP VP-complements.

We see then that the standard and extended standard theories not only must contend with examples such as (1b), (2b), and (3b), but that the means that these theories employ to avoid such examples amounts to a loss of generalization inasmuch as the constraints proposed to rule out such examples do not generalize with mechanisms proposed to rule out examples such as (5a–c). By contrast, the approach that I have advocated, cf. Brame [2], avoids the ill-formed examples in a general, straightforward way. Predicates such as *try* select VP-complements and predicates such as *want* and *persuade* select NP VP-complements.

Such an approach has further consequences. Consider the well-known problem of the following examples:

(6) a. Who do you want ____ to see John?
   b. *Who do you wanna see John?

As has been pointed out often, reduction and contraction are prohibited in the presence of a removal site as in (6b). Now, if there is indeed a rule of Equi, we would expect (7b) to be ill-formed just as in (6b).

(7) a. Do you want ____ to sleep?
    b. Do you wanna sleep?

But (7b) is fully grammatical, suggesting that no equi-NP was in fact present in the structure underlying (7b). Consequently, we are led to conclude that there is no rule Equi. It then follows without theoretical elaboration that (7b) is possible, whereas (6b) is not, since there is no removal site in the case of (7b), as opposed to (6b), which does exhibit a removal site. This explanation strikes me as natural and straightforward. It requires no theoretical subtlety. It demands no theoretical elaboration to write off (7b) as counterevidence. Things follow without employment of theoretical prophylactic. It is the difference between an explanation and a description.

There are some important consequences of our conclusion that Equi does not exist. Consider the following examples:

(8) a. Mary was examined by the doctor.
    b. Mary tried to be examined by the doctor.

(9) a. They expected Jimmy to rip us off.
    b. Jimmy was expected by them to rip us off.

It is generally assumed that (8a) derives from its active counterpart via a transformation called Passive. But consider the derivation of (8b).

(10) a. Mary tried [$_s$ the doctor to examine Mary]$_s$ $\Rightarrow$ Passive

     b. Mary tried [$_s$ Mary to be examined by the doctor]$_s$ $\Rightarrow$ Equi

     c. Mary tried ____ to be examined by the doctor

To derive (8b), utilizing the Passive transformation, we arrive at stage (b) of (10), which requires Equi to derive the desired results. Thus, if Passive exists, then Equi exists. But we have concluded that Equi does not exist. Therefore, we must conclude that Passive does not exist. It follows, then, that passive structures, like VP structures, should be generated directly. This is not at all an undesirable consequence. In fact, if passives are generated directly, there is no need for an agent-deletion transformation since agents need not be generated at all by base structures, cf. [2: 133].

Let us now turn to (9a) and (9b). Examples such as (9a) are

generally derived by a transformation that raises the NP subject of the complement into the object position of the matrix S. Let us call this putative rule, Raising to Object Position, or ROP for short. Notice that ROP is also utilized in deriving (9b). The requisite derivation is given in (11).

(11) They expected [$_S$ Jimmy to rip us off]$_S$ $\implies$ ROP

They expected Jimmy [$_S$ to rip us off]$_S$ $\implies$ Passive

Jimmy was expected by them to rip us off

Thus, if we assume that there is a rule of ROP, then we need Passive to yield the desired results in (11). But there is no rule of Passive because there is no Equi. Consequently there is no ROP.

Similar conclusions can be reached for other transformations that do not make essential use of variables, what I will call *local transformations*. Thus, consider the following examples:

(12) a. Mary tried to appear to be calm.
     b. Every child was given a dime.
     c. He tried to be easy to please.
     d. There was believed to be jelly between his toes.

By reasoning completely analogous to the foregoing, it is possible to conclude on the basis of such examples that there are no rules such as Raising to Subject Position (hereafter RSP), Dative, and *there*-Insertion. Thus, consider (12a), on the assumption that RSP applies in the course of its derivation.

(13) a. Mary tried [$_S$ it to appear [$_S$ Mary to be calm]] $\implies$ RSP
     b. Mary tried [$_S$ Mary to appear [$_S$ to be calm]] $\implies$ Equi
     c. Mary tried ____ to appear to be calm

Again, we see, quite clearly, that Equi is a consequence of RSP for such examples. Thus, if we are to maintain our assumption that there is no rule of Equi, then we must also give up RSP and search for an alternative account of the range of data that it explains. Or, turning to (12b), under the assumption that Dative moves an NP leftward, we obtain the following derivation:

(14) a. Δ gave a dime to every child $\implies$ Dative
     b. Δ gave every child a dime $\implies$ Passive (and Δ-deletion)
     c. Every child was given a dime.

Here we see that if Dative applies to (14a) to yield (14b), then Passive must subsequently apply so as to derive (14c). But we previously concluded that Passive does not exist since Equi does not exist. Hence if Dative is contingent on Passive, there can be no Dative in the form assumed for this derivation. And likewise for Object-Shift. Thus, consider the derivation associated with (12c).

(15) a. He$_i$ tried [$_S$ it to be easy [$_S$ Δ to please he$_i$] ⟹ Object-Shift
   b. He$_i$ tried [$_S$ he$_i$ to be easy [$_S$ Δ to please] ⟹ Equi
   c. He tried ____ to be easy to please

After Object-Shift has applied to yield (15b), Equi is needed to provide for the desired surface structure. Thus, Object-Shift must be eliminated also if Equi is given up. And, finally, it is possible to arrive at a similar conclusion with respect to *there*-Insertion, as indicated in the derivation of (12d).

(16) a. Δ believed [$_S$ jelly to be between his toes] ⟹ *there*-Insertion
   b. Δ believed [$_S$ there to be jelly between his toes] ⟹ ROP
   c. Δ believed there [$_S$ to be jelly between his toes] ⟹ Passive
   d. There was believed to be jelly between his toes.

Derivation (16) illustrates a contingency of *there*-Insertion on ROP and Passive, which, recall, do not exist if Equi does not exist. Proceeding on the assumption that Equi does not exist, we conclude that *there*-Insertion does not either.

   Thus, we see that the consequences of giving up Equi are somewhat drastic. One could perhaps take these conclusions as a *reductio ad absurdum* argument against abandoning Equi, but I will accept the correct alternative hypothesis and assume that all structures previously derived by local transformations must in fact be generated as base structures. Let us call this approach the base hypothesis.

   Base Hypothesis:
   All structures previously derived by local transformations are in fact generated by phrase structure rules.

The base hypothesis was first advanced in the course of my Fulbright-Hays lectures at the Rijksuniversiteit te Utrecht in the fall of 1973 and later published as [2]. If one accepts the base hypothesis, the interesting question of just what is to replace the traditional local transformations arises. I will have more to say concerning this question below. First, however, I wish to provide several additional arguments to support the base hypothesis.

2. AFFIX-HOPPING AND *there*-Insertion

In this section new evidence will be adduced to support the base hypothesis. First, let us consider the putative rule known as Affix-Hopping, which was initially proposed and formulated in Chomsky [10],[11]. The key fact is that Affix-Hopping is a local transformation in our sense. That is, it does not make essential use of variables and, therefore, according to the base hypothesis, is not a transformation. There is, in fact, some evidence indicating that auxiliaries can be generated in English directly by base rules and that direct generation is desirable. This approach makes use of a more sophisticated theory of the lexicon, one promising approach being that developed in Hust [21],[22].

By way of presenting the evidence, let us note first that the standard theory misses a significant generalization. Consider, for example, the following ungrammatical cases:

(17) a. *John is being drinking beer.
    b. *John's being drinking beer all day surprises me.
    c. *Being drinking beer all day, John is slowly going under.

Consider first (17a). How is this example prohibited within the framework of the standard theory? It is blocked by virtue of the phrase structure rules expanding Aux, as in (18).

(18)   Aux $\longrightarrow$ tense (M) (have en) (be ing)

Since two instances of *be ing* cannot be generated by rule (18), example (17a) will never arise subsequent to Affix-Hopping. Thus, one mechanism, namely, phrase structure, is utilized to block (17a). However, a totally different mechanism must be utilized to block (17b) and (17c), since presumably the gerundive and participial phrases in such examples are derived via transformation from sentential sources in the standard theory. In fact, Chomsky quite explicitly remarks that examples such as (17b) are blocked by a special constraint:

> (19)   Forms such as *John's being reading the book* (but not *John's having been reading the book*) are blocked by a restriction against certain *-ing -ing* sequences (compare *John's stopping reading, John's having stopped reading,* etc.)   [14:16, note 6]

Thus, examples (17b) and (17c) are ruled out by a special restriction on *-ing -ing* sequences, constituting one mechanism, whereas example (17a) is ruled out by a totally different mechanism, phrase structure. This amounts to a loss of generalization. The significant generalization for all the examples appears to be that *being* does not select *-ing*-complements. This generalization could be expressed if *being* were a lexical item, but it goes unexpressed under the traditional approach utilizing Affix-Hopping.

I will sketch briefly and tentatively one possible lexical approach below. But first let us turn to a second set of examples which bears on the base hypothesis.

(20) a. There was a boy being arrested.
    b. *There was being a boy arrested.
    c. There were to be three boys arrested.

Examples such as these pose critical problems for the standard theory of transformational grammar, where expletive *there* is inserted via transformation. Within such an approach adopting *there*-Insertion, special conditions and complications must be associated with this rule in order to keep it from applying so as to provide (20b). It might be asked how such restrictions could correctly prohibit (20b) and yet allow (20c). If we assume that such restrictions are, in fact, formulable so as to account for the data in (20), we must still conclude that such an account leads to a loss of significant generalization inasmuch as it fails to provide a general account of the examples in (20) and those in (21).

(21) a. It was a boy being arrested.
    b. *It was being a boy arrested.
    c. It was to be a boy arrested.

Apparently (21b) must be ruled out by a mechanism completely independent of *there*-Insertion, if *there* is inserted transformationally in (20). However, the correct approach would utilize the same mechanism to rule out (21b) and (20b). This mechanism entails generating existential sentences directly. It thereby supports the base hypothesis which provides for direct generation of existentials.

A tentative account of the data can be sketched by making use of Hust's theory of the lexicon along with a version of Emonds' approach to auxiliaries in English. Tentative phrase structure rules are provided in (22).

(22) a. S̄ ⟶ Comp S
    b. S ⟶ NP Aux VP
    c. VP ⟶ V VP . . .
    d. Aux ⟶ tense (M)

PS rules

Lexical entries are represented as trees and lexical items are taken to be individual leaves of lexical trees. By Hust's precipitation convention, "all features of a node A in a lexical entry are assigned to all nodes dominated by A" [21: 51]. Thus, a simplified representation for *refuse* ~ *refusal* is, according to Hust, the following:

(23)

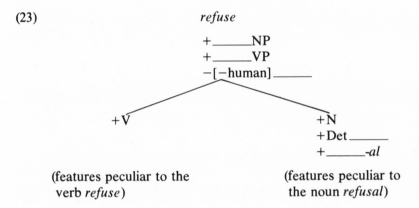

                          refuse

                +_____NP
                +_____VP
             −[−human]_____

+V̄   +N
                                 +Det_____
                               +_____-*al*

(features peculiar to the   (features peculiar to
  verb *refuse*)   the noun *refusal*)

Hust supplements his lexicon with a set of redundancy rules, as suggested by Chomsky in earlier work. Thus, for example, +N in (23) can be filled in by redundancy rules on the basis of the presence of the feature +Det_____. It is to be emphasized that individual lexical items are leaves of trees such as (23). Together with the precipitation convention, then, a lexical entry will be a constellation of syntactic and phonological (and perhaps semantic) features. It is to be noted that morphological features such as +_____-*al* in (23) are considered to be part of the lexical entry itself after feature precipitation (as opposed to a context for lexical insertion). Thus, the lexical entry for *refusal*, after precipitation, is [+_____NP, +_____VP, −[−human]_____, +N, +Det_____] together with the phonological sequence *refusal*.

    A similar approach can now be taken in the case of auxiliary elements in English. It will be assumed that active participles such as *eating, having, being,* etc., are dominated by the category V̄, that past participles such as *eaten, had, been,* etc., are dominated by the category $\overline{\overline{V}}$, and that nonderived verbs such as *eat, have, be,* etc., are dominated by V. This elaboration entails a slight modification of rule (22c).

(24)   VP $\longrightarrow$ $\begin{Bmatrix} V \\ \overline{V} \\ \overline{\overline{V}} \end{Bmatrix}$ VP . . .

The lexical entry for *eat* and its related participles can now be tentatively given as follows:

(25)   *eat*

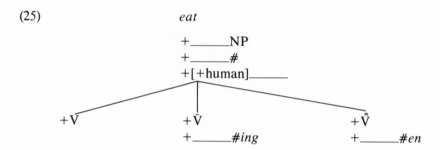

$$+\underline{\qquad}NP$$
$$+\underline{\qquad}\#$$
$$+[+human]\underline{\qquad}$$

$+\overline{V}$ $+\overline{V}$ $+\overline{\overline{V}}$
$+\underline{\qquad}\#ing$ $+\underline{\qquad}\#en$

Actually, (25) is redundant in various ways. For example, the participial endings can be omitted provided we supplement the lexicon with the following redundancy rules[2]:

(26) $[+\overline{V}] \longrightarrow [+\underline{\qquad}\#ing]$
        $[+\overline{\overline{V}}] \longrightarrow [+\underline{\qquad}\#en]$

Thus, *eat, eating,* and *eaten* are all considered to be individual *lexical items,* although the fact that all three select complements is expressed in terms of a single *lexical entry.* That is, the precipitation convention will associate the relevant contextual features of the root node of (25) with its leaves.

Now let us consider how the correct order of auxiliaries is predicted within the approach sketched here. In this case, *be* can be given the tentative representation in (27).

---

[2] Many details and redundant properties of lexical items are being glossed over here in order to avoid unduly burdening the exposition. For example, irregular past participles are listed ad hoc and cannot be predicted, whereas the feature $+\overline{V}$ for present participles is itself redundant. A detailed discussion of these and other properties of the auxiliary system in English is provided in Brame [4].

(27)

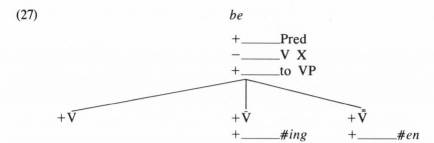

Of interest here is the feature [−_____V X]. This feature will prohibit sequences such as *John was eat the beans* but will allow *John was eating the beans* and *John was seen.* Thus, *be* can be followed by active and passive participles. This is also true of *been,* as predicted by feature precipitation.

(28) a. *John has *been eat* the beans.
    b. John has *been eating* the beans.
    c. John has *been seen.*

Likewise, by feature precipitation we expect a similar state of affairs to hold for *being.*

(29) a. *John is *being eat* the beans.
    b. *John is *being eating* the beans.
    c. John is *being taken.*

Of course, the fact that (29b) is ungrammatical is just the problem described earlier in terms of (17a). But, now, we may account for (29b)-(17a), as well as (17b) and (17c) with one general redundancy rule.

(30) $[+\bar{V}] \longrightarrow [-\underline{\hspace{1.5em}}\bar{V}\ X]$

This rule may be taken as a formalization of Chomsky's restriction noted in (19); however, by giving up Affix-Hopping and by treating the distribution of auxiliaries lexically, we succeed in expressing all of the facts in (17) by the same means, namely, by (31), whereas the standard theory, it will be recalled, requires two separate mechanisms.[3]

---

[3] The so-called doubl-ing facts have been discussed by Ross [35], who proposes a global rule to account for the relevant data. Both Emonds [17] and Milsark [30] have demonstrated that a nonglobal account is superior. Pullum [32] has adduced new evidence. In Brame [4] the controversy is reviewed and it is shown that the doubl-ing facts all follow naturally from an approach similar to that advanced here, i.e., from a more sophisticated theory of the lexicon together with redundancy rules.

Let us now also return to (20b) and (21b). Recall that the standard theory must rule out (20b) by constraining *there*-Insertion without, however, blocking (20c), and it must rule out (20b) by a different mechanism since *there*-Insertion is irrelevant in this case. It can now be shown that both of these examples, (20b) and (21b), can be ruled out by a natural extension of the redundancy rule (30) and that, consequently, there is indeed a deeper generalization missed by the standard theory.

Let us assume that Pred is expanded according to rule (31).[4]

$$(31) \quad \text{Pred} \longrightarrow (\text{NP}) \begin{Bmatrix} \text{VP} \\ \text{PP} \\ \text{AP} \\ \text{A}_{\text{SD}} \end{Bmatrix}$$

Let us assume further that expletive *there* is generated directly in subject position by base rules and that there is no rule of *there*-Insertion. Then (20a) and (21a) are allowed by virtue of the lexical entry for *be* in (27). The same distribution should hold for *being* and *been*. However, in the case of *being*, as in (20b) and (21b), the presence of Pred leads to ungrammaticality. But now we may simply extend the redundancy rule (30) in the following way:

$$(32) \quad [+\bar{\text{V}}] \longrightarrow [-\underline{\quad}\bar{\text{V}} \text{ X}, -\underline{\quad}\text{Pred}]$$

Thus, by (32), active participles, in particular *being*, will select neither active participles nor predicate phrases as their complements. This analysis thus succeeds in ruling out (20b) in precisely the same way that it rules out (21b), a generalization missed in the standard theory. This mechanism, it will be recalled, also accounts for the examples laid out in (17).

Additional examples, brought to my attention by Robin Cooper, make it necessary to further revise (32). These examples include the following:

(33) a. I do not approve of there being two knives on the table.
   b. There being nobody at home, we left.

Such examples show that the prohibition against predicate comple-

---

[4] Rule (31) is tentative and by no means exhausts the predicate phrase, which has been neglected in transformational studies. The inclusion of (NP) within the Pred phrase may be incorrect, as assumed in [31].

ments is not absolute in the case of active participles, but rather contingent on the presence of an overt auxiliary element such as *tense* or *modal*. Therefore, it is necessary to alter (32) so as to express this fact.

(34) $[+\bar{V}] \longrightarrow [-\_\_\_\bar{V}$ X, $-$NP Aux$\_\_\_$Pred]

It thus appears that a number of facts can be handled adequately within the framework advanced here. The generalizations that emerge, however, depend crucially on existential sentences being base generated. This is a conclusion reached on independent grounds in section 1, a conclusion which is consistent with the base hypothesis and argued independently in Jenkins [24] and Brame [2].[5] The data adduced in this section therefore support this hypothesis.

Before turning to additional evidence for base generated structures previously derived by transformation, let us consider the following examples mentioned in Akmajian and Wasow [1] and elaborated in Iwakura [23].

---

[5] It was Emonds [15] who first noted and attempted to come to grips with examples such as the following:

(i) a.   Some boys were doctors.
     b.   *There were some boys doctors.
(ii) a.   An elephant was small.
     b.   *There was an elephant small.

Emonds' explanation was based on structural considerations and the structure-preserving hypothesis. To create the ungrammatical (b) examples required a violation of the structure-preserving hypothesis, which is possible only in the case of root transformations (and minor movement rules) within Emonds' framework. Jenkins [25] attempted to account for the same phenomena utilizing Emonds' basic observation concerning phrase structure. However, for Jenkins, expletive *there* is base generated with no rule of *there*-Insertion. Thus, the (b) examples could not arise because the phrase structure rules could not give rise to the relevant structures. Recently, Milsark [31] has, perceptively, noted that some analogous sentences are well-formed.

(iii) a.   (All over the world) there are people hungry.
      b.   (After the banquet) there were several people sick.

Milsark indicates that such examples tend to argue against base generated existentials; however, such a conclusion does not appear to me to follow. Milsark divides the adjectives into two classes: those that permit *there* as in (iii), which he calls *state-descriptive* (SD), and those that do not as in (ii), which he calls *property* (P) predicates. This distribution is reflected in rule (31) of the text by the inclusion of A_{SD}, signifying the class of state-descriptive adjectives. However, Milsark considers the distinction to be semantic in nature. If it is, there is no reason why the semantic explanation cannot be expressed in terms of the base generated structures in the absence of a rule of *there*-Insertion. Thus, I can see no way in which such examples argue against base generated existentials.

(35) a. Sam was being examined by a psychiatrist and Bill was
_____ too.
  b. *Sam was being examined by a psychiatrist and Bill was being
_____ too.

Akmajian and Wasow fail to express a basic generalization concerning the full range of relevant examples involving VP phenomena, as Iwakura [23] shows. However, Iwakura also fails to express the generalization since he requires at least two mechanisms to rule out the structures which would otherwise be generated. Thus, for Iwakura (35b) is prohibited because *examined by a psychiatrist* is not a single VP constituent within his framework, an assumption which can be questioned, and (36) is prohibited because of a special condition which he associates with VP-Deletion.

(36) *Which bothers you more: John's having taken a drug, or Bill's having _____?

If we consider VP gaps to be base generated as such, both (35b) and (36) can be ruled out by the same means. We need only revise the redundancy rule (34) so that *being* will not select the empty context.

(37) $[+\bar{V}] \longrightarrow [-\_\_\_\bar{V} \ X, \ -NP \ Aux\_\_\_Pred, \ -\_\_\_]$

If this approach is correct, it shows that VP's should not be deleted, as assumed in early studies. Rather, VP phenomena must be treated interpretively as argued in some recent work. Moreover, this conclusion has consequences which bear on the base hypothesis, for consider the examples listed in (38).

(38) a. They said that Mary appears to be sick, and she does _____.
  b. Joe was examined by a quack and Bill was _____ too.
  c. They said there was an elephant in the yard and there was
_____.
  d. Mary was given a message and Sue was _____ too.

According to the approach advocated here, the gaps in (38a–d) are base generated. But if this is indeed the case, then Raising to Subject Position, Passive, *there*-Insertion, and Dative cannot account for the data exhibited in the right conjunct of each of these examples. Thus, the relevant structures must be based generated, a conclusion arrived at on independent grounds in section 1.

3. EXTRAPOSITION AND SENTENTIAL SUBJECTS

In the foregoing it has been suggested that structures previously derived by local transformations are in fact base generated. By local transformations is meant transformations which do not make essential use of variables. Now what about the putative rule of Extraposition? This transformation has been stated with variables in the literature of transformational grammar. However, there is an important difference between Extraposition and other rules stated with variables, such as Question Formation, Relative Clause Formation, Topicalization, etc. For, the variable in Extraposition could in principle be replaced by a disjunction of constant terms, although such is not the case for Question Formation, Relative Clause Formation, etc. To put it differently, in Ross's terms, Extraposition is bounded, whereas the other rules mentioned are not.

Now, if we take essential variable to mean unbounded essential variable of the type found in Question Formation, Relative Clause Formation, etc., then Extraposition is a local transformation in the relevant sense and, therefore, accepting the base hypothesis, should not be considered a transformation. Rather, extraposed S's should be base generated and sentential subject S's should also be base generated. This position is taken in Brame [2: 142].

Let us now turn to some evidence which supports the base generation hypothesis in this case. First, it is important to observe that S's and VP's are not NP's, a position defended in Emonds [15],[16] on the basis of examples such as the following[6]:

(39) a. *They told *that everything would turn out for the best* to the children.
   b. They told the children *that everything would turn out for the best*.
   c. They told *a story* to the children.
   d. They told the children *a story*.

(40) a. *He blamed it on *that Bill was too strict*.
   b. He blamed it on *Bill's strictness*.

(41) a. *It was *that John refused to see the light* that bothered us.
   b. It was *John's refusal* that bothered us.

[6] Emonds' correct assumptions concerning the non-NP nature of sentential complements are questioned in Higgins [19] and Horn [20]. The relevant arguments are refuted in Brame [4]. Emonds himself abandoned his analysis of the relevant examples in [18] for an inferior analysis. See [4] for discussion and arguments against Emonds' more recent analysis.

(42) a. *You promised *to be quiet* to Mary.
   b. You promised Mary *to be quiet*.
   c. You promised *a new hat* to Mary.
   d. You promised Mary *a new hat*.

These data indicate that S's and VP's are not NP's since they would be expected to exhibit the identical distribution of NP's if they were. Thus, in (39c), the true NP *a story* can occupy the immediate postverbal slot in the sentence, but this is not so in the case of (39a), indicating that the italicized phrase is not an NP, etc.

Let us accept Emonds' straightforward explanation for this range of data and proceed now to the crucial examples.

(43) a. That John was sick bothered Mary.
   b. *Did that John was sick bother Mary?

(44) a. That John dislikes artichokes surprised you.
   b. *Which artichokes did that John dislikes surprise you?

(45) a. That it bothers the teacher for John to smoke is quite possible.
   b. *That for John to smoke bothers the teacher is quite possible.

(46) a. That he forgot his lesson proves that John was not serious.
   b. *It proves that John was not serious that he forgot his lesson.

These examples have been discussed and treated by grammarians working within the transformational framework. The grammarians include Ross [35], Emonds [15],[18], Higgins [19], Kuno [27], Horn [20], and Iwakura [24]. It seems to me that all of the analyses advanced have failed in one way or another to express the basic generalization underlying the full range of data.[7] Accepting the base hypothesis, we can attempt to express the generalization in terms of phrase structure.

Let us recall that in Emonds' earlier work [15: 69], it was argued that sentential subjects are not dominated by NP in surface structure. Thus, Emonds argued that an example such as *For the house to be painted would irritate him* should be represented in surface structure as (47).

---

[7] It should be noted that although I disagree with Iwakura's ingenious analysis in [24], he was the first to recognize that there is indeed a deeper generalization to be expressed. Iwakura also provides much penetrating criticism of Horn [20].

(47)

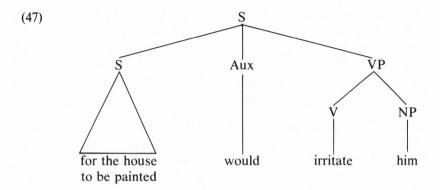

According to Emonds [15], (47) is derived by a rule which is essentially the inverse of Extraposition, where S is substituted for the NP subject. However, adopting the base hypothesis, let us now assume that Emonds' surface structure is in fact the base generated structure.[8] That is, let us assume that S's and VP's can be generated directly as subjects where the relevant categories are not dominated by NP. To resolve the difficulties that arise in connection with (43)–(46), however, let us introduce the category $\bar{\bar{S}}$, which will play a crucial role in explaining the relevant data.

(48) a. $\bar{\bar{S}} \longrightarrow \left\{ \begin{matrix} \bar{S} \\ VP \end{matrix} \right\}$ Aux VP

   b. $\bar{S} \longrightarrow$ Comp S

   c. $S \longrightarrow$ NP Aux VP

   d. $VP \longrightarrow V \left\{ \begin{matrix} \bar{\bar{S}} \\ \bar{S} \\ VP \\ . \\ . \\ . \end{matrix} \right\} \ldots$

Now let us see how this reanalysis explains all of the data tabulated in (43)–(46) without recourse to special constraints such as Ross's Sentential Subject Constraint and Island Internal S Constraint, Emonds' prohibition against multiple application of root transformations, Horn's NP Constraint and global Pruning, etc.

---

[8] Alfredo Hurtado has informed me that he also has made this assumption for the grammar of Spanish.

Consider first (43b). Since *that John was sick* is a sentential subject, Comp is unavailable for the root S̄ which dominates it, and consequently a question cannot be formed. For exactly the same reason, a *wh*-question cannot be formed and thus (44b) cannot be derived. Example (45b) also cannot be generated since the sentential subject S̄ cannot be expanded to yield a second sentential subject by rule (48b). Finally, (46b) is avoided by virtue of the fact that VP cannot be expanded by rule (48d) so as to provide two sentential complements. In sum, we see that all of the relevant examples are explained quite naturally by phrase structure. This analysis should be compared with the existing proposals of the literature mentioned above.

Additional support for the position outlined here is gleaned from the following examples.

(49) a. I imagine for one to work that hard would require a lot of effort.
   b. I suppose to do that would require a good deal of manual dexterity.
   c. I guess that the night is black demonstrates that the universe is expanding.
   d. I imagine that Bill works hard shows that he is German.

Many speakers apparently accept some sentences such as these with embedded sentential and VP subjects, although there is variation from speaker to speaker. Other examples are clearly ungrammatical for all speakers.

(50) a. *I resent for you to leave would bother her.
   b. *It is surprising for you to say that would annoy him.
   c. *It bothers me that John left proves that he was not serious.

The fact that we do obtain different results for different predicates, say *imagine* vs. *resent,* indicates that we are dealing with a lexical phenomenon, i.e., with subcategorization. But the reanalysis sketched out in the foregoing makes just such an approach possible since rule (48d) has been introduced to provide for S̄. Thus, *imagine, guess,* etc., but not *resent,* etc. can be subcategorized so as to select S̄, providing for (49a–d), but not for (50a–c).

The new analysis makes a further prediction which is borne out. It predicts a contrast between the examples laid out in (51) and those listed in (49).

(51) a. *I imagine that for one to work that hard would require a lot of effort.
     b. *I suppose that to do that would require a good deal of manual dexterity.
     c. *I guess that that the night is black demonstrates that the universe is expanding.
     d. *I imagine that that Bill works hard shows that he is German.

These data follow from the fact that S̿ does not directly dominate a Comp node as does S̄. Hence, the complementizers such as *that* and *for* in (49) are all associated with the sentential S̄ which is dominated by S̿. This explanation appears to be quite natural and straightforward. If correct, it should lend credence to the analysis advanced in this section.

4.   THE SPELLING PROHIBITION

In sections 3 and 4, new evidence has been provided to support base generated structures which were previously derived via transformation. In this section a general constraint will be suggested which has the effect of favoring the analyses outlined above. The Spelling Prohibition will, in fact, have the effect of prohibiting the previous transformational analyses which have been impugned by the evidence adduced in the previous discussion. This constraint can be initially formulated as follows.

Spelling Prohibition (weak form):
Transformations cannot spell out morphological material (or effect the spelling out).

The effect of the Spelling Prohibition is to ensure that all morphological material is present after lexical insertion. Thus, the presence of morphological material such as the expletive *there* and the passive *be en* is contingent on phrase structure and the lexicon, a result which is consistent with the arguments of previous sections. Consequently, the Spelling Prohibition makes classical transformations such as *there*-Insertion and Passive unavailable to the theory, a desirable result.

The Spelling Prohibition has consequences for many other transformations proposed in the literature of transformational grammar. For one, it disallows a rule switching *some* to *any* as suggested in earlier work such as Klima [26]. Rather, *any* must be introduced directly into phrase structure. That there is no rule turning *some* to *any* has been argued in Lakoff [29].[9] Another proposed transformation which is prohibited by the Spelling Prohibition is Comp-Placement, which was originally proposed in Rosenbaum [34]. The fact that Bresnan [5],[7] has shown that complementizers such as *that, for,* and *wh* must be present in phrase structure shows that the Spelling Prohibition (hereafter SP) makes a correct prediction in this case. SP also rules out the possibility of deriving NP's such as *John's picture* from relative clause constructions such as *the picture that John has* as proposed in early work and accepted in Chomsky [14: 40 *passim*] and suggests base generation as per the base generated possessives involving intrinsic connection discussed by Chomsky. This follows from the fact that the morphological material *'s* would otherwise have to be spelled out by the transformation. Other elements are also prohibited as transformationally inserted elements, such as the *of* in *several of John's proofs of the theorem,* cf. Chomsky [14: 53]. Bresnan has in fact suggested that *of* should not be inserted by transformation; cf. [8]. Again we see that SP makes the correct prediction. SP likewise prohibits deriving *who, what,* etc., from *wh-someone, wh-something,* etc., as argued in Chomsky [12]. Chomsky has shown that *who* and *someone, what* and *something,* etc., bear a close relationship in that they exhibit many distributional similarities, one illustration of which is given in (52).

(52) a. Harry will meet with someone else.
b. Who else will Harry meet with?
c. *Harry will meet with a girl else.
d. *Harry will meet with the adviser else.

In (52) we see that *else* can co-occur with *wh*-words and with *some*-words. This fact could be explained if *who, what,* etc., derived from *wh-someone, wh-something,* etc. However, SP disallows such a derivation, and therefore we might expect to find a difference in distributional properties. We do indeed find a distinguishing environment.

(53) a. *Who the hell* broke my typewriter?
b. **Someone the hell* broke my typewriter.

---

[9] This point holds for the general process of Negative Incorporation proposed by Klima, Ross, and others. For a discussion of how examples such as *John has any money* are to be blocked, see [3] and [4].

(54) a. *What in tarnation* are you talking about?
   b. *You are talking about *something in tarnation*.

(55) a. *Where in the name of God* did Sam buy that Okito box?   (≠)
   b. *Sam bought that Okito box *somewhere in the name of God*.

Such examples again show that SP makes correct predictions. Proceeding, we see that SP also disallows *do*-Support as a transformation in any of the variant formulations in which *do* is inserted by transformation. Rather, according to SP, *do* must be introduced in base structures. Rules such as Case-Marking, Subject-Verb Agreement, and other agreement rules are also prohibited by SP. Rather, case violations, agreement violations, and the like should apparently be treated by a checking or filtering mechanism, as suggested in Bresnan [12: note 8] and Brame [3]. The classical approach to pronominalization and reflexivization is also disallowed by SP. This accords with much recent research which shows that pronouns, reflexives, and reciprocals should be base generated. Base generation of such pronouns and anaphoric pronouns, including *so*, is a direct consequence of SP, thus lending further credence to its correctness. Finally, SP has the virtue of prohibiting lexical decomposition, which plays a prominent role in generative semantics. Thus, for example, Seuren writes that generative semanticists "posit a great deal of transformational syntax inside, or behind, lexical items, especially verbs" [37: 5]; advocates of this lexical decomposition approach derive the (b) examples of (56)–(59) from structures akin to the corresponding (a) examples.

(56) a. John struck Bill as being similar to a gorilla.
   b. Bill reminded John of a gorilla.

(57) a. The sauce came to be thick.
   b. The sauce thickened.

(58) a. John caused Harry to die.
   b. John killed Harry.

(59) a. Mary persuaded Bill not to go.
   b. Mary dissuaded Bill from going.

Considerable language-internal evidence has been adduced in [2: Chap. 1] to demonstrate that lexical decomposition cannot be maintained without loss of significant generalization. The fact that SP is consistent with these language-specific independent arguments further supports it as a basic constraint on the functioning of grammars.

It is possible, and quite conceivably correct, to strengthen SP in the following way:

> *Spelling Prohibition* (strong form):
> Transformations cannot spell out or alter morphological material.

The strong form of SP has the added effect of prohibiting deletion of morphological material as well as substitution for morphological material. Thus, substitution of a sentential complement for *it*, according to one version of Raising to Subject Position and Raising to Object Position is prohibited, a result consistent with the conclusions of section 1. Similarly, Object-Shift, which substitutes an object NP for *it* so as to derive sentences such as *John is easy to please* from *it is easy to please John* is disallowed, a result which again coincides with the conclusions of section 1. Of course, the deletion approach to Object-Shift phenomena, as proposed in [30], is also prohibited by the strong form of SP; cf. [2] for discussion. The strong form of SP also disallows Extraposition, albeit somewhat indirectly, since *it*-Deletion is prohibited. Alternative approaches involving spelling out of *it*, as in [18], are ruled out by the weak form of SP. Dative is also disallowed since deletion of *to* or *for* is ruled out, as are alternative approaches which spell out *to* and *for*. Finally, the deletion approach to VP gaps is also ruled out by the strong form of SP.

We see, then, that SP has consequences consistent with the language-internal arguments advanced in [2] and in the preceding sections. This convergence provides considerable motivation for SP and, therefore, it is advanced as a universal constraint on the functioning of transformations.

5. LEXICALISM VS. THE INVERSE CYCLE

In view of the fact that a large number of transformations must be abandoned in favor of base generated structures, we might ask just how the explanations provided by the classical transformations are to be expressed. Before attempting an answer to this question, it is important to recognize just what it is that the classical transformations account for since there is a good deal of misunderstanding on this point. Let us take Passive as the basis of discussion in this section.

It is often asserted that transformational rules account for paraphrase relations or synonymy relations which hold between the sentences related by transformation. The truth is that paraphrase and synonymy remain as vague today as they were before the advent of transformational grammar. Transformations provide no insights into and shed no light on putative relations such as paraphrase and synonymy. Others have argued that grammatical relations are preserved under transformation, yet such advocates fail to indicate to what extent such relations yield insight into any interesting questions or how they resolve outstanding issues. It seems, therefore, that we must recognize that classical transformations have served one and only one basic function, and that is the syntactic function of accounting for distributional generalizations by avoiding repetitive statements involving co-occurrence phenomena.[10] For example, in the case of Passive, it has been assumed that if an active verb selects an NP as direct object, its passive counterpart will select that NP as subject. And if an active verb does not select an NP as object or fails to select a specific kind of NP as object, then the same facts will hold for the subject of the passive counterpart. Thus, because (60a) allows *the beans* as object of *eat*, (60b) allows *the beans* as subject of *be eaten*. And, equally important, because (61a) does not allow *sincerity* as object of *sleep*, *sincerity* is not allowed as subject of *be slept*.

(60) a. John ate the beans.
   b. The beans were eaten by John.

(61) a. John slept sincerity.
   b. Sincerity was slept by John.

Since the foregoing is a distributional argument, it is quite obviously a syntactic argument. Now, if passives are derived from actives, then the convergence of distributional facts follows as a consequence and need be stated only once in the grammar, namely, before the Passive rule applies. However, if Passive is abandoned in its classical formulation, then how can the syntactic generalizations be expressed? One answer to this question was provided in Brame [2], where both actives and passives are base generated in conformity with the base hypothesis of section 1. In lieu of the classical rule of Passive, its inverse was proposed which had the effect of converting base generated passives into structures identical to actives. It was at this deep level of derived actives that the co-occurrence restrictions were checked, thus expressing the basic generalization inherent in (60)–(61).

Another possibility was suggested in earlier work: "Granted that passives are generated directly, it remains to relate them to corresponding actives. One approach would be to formulate a lexical redundancy rule taking a form quite similar to the Passive transforma-

---

[10] Excellent discussion of this point can be found in Hust [21].

tion itself" [2: 132][11]. Recently Bresnan [9] has provided an explicit statement of such a redundancy rule and has suggested that all local transformations be supplanted by lexical redundancy rules, thus accepting the base hypothesis. Let us identify the redundancy rule approach with the lexicalist hypothesis which was initiated in Chomsky [14]. This position can be informally stated in a strong form as follows:

Lexicalist Hypothesis:
All co-occurrence generalizations previously expressed by local transformations are expressed by lexical redundancy rules.

The inverse cycle and the lexicalist hypothesis are contrasted schematically in (62).

(62)   INVERSE CYCLE

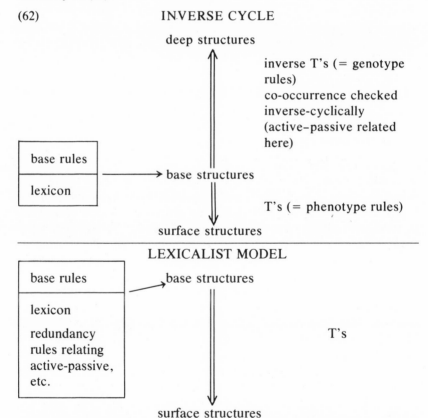

deep structures

inverse T's (= genotype rules)
co-occurrence checked inverse-cyclically
(active–passive related here)

base rules

lexicon

base structures

T's (= phenotype rules)

surface structures

LEXICALIST MODEL

base rules

base structures

lexicon

redundancy rules relating active-passive, etc.

T's

surface structures

---

[11] Several classical transformations were formulated as redundancy rules during the course of my Fulbright-Hays lectures at the Rijksuniversiteit te Utrecht in 1973; however, the project was terminated by my failure to work out the relevant facts concerning Equi.

There is a certain naturalness to the lexicalist model depicted in (62). Local transformations are typically local by virtue of the fact that a particular lexical item, usually a predicate, serves as the locus of the transformation. It is quite natural to express the locality of such phenomena in that area of the grammar where lexical items are represented and where unboundedness cannot be expressed, namely, in the lexicon. Then, it is no longer a mystery why certain lexical items typically serve as the locus of local transformations.

Now, however, we must ask if there are any empirical arguments favoring one approach over the other. In the case of Passive, there appears to be some evidence favoring the lexicalist model. To see this, let us return to the lexical entry for *eat* as (25) in section 2. By feature precipitation, the past participle *eaten* will be positively specified for +_____NP, whereas the NP object must assume the subject position in this case, in fact. Otherwise, a grammar incorporating (25), along with base generated past participles, will give rise to ungrammatical strings such as *NP was eaten the bananas*. To overcome this difficulty, just as we posited lexical redundancy rule (34) to account for additional distributional characteristics of $\bar{V}$, we may now do likewise for $\bar{\bar{V}}$.[12]

(63) $[+\bar{\bar{V}}] \longrightarrow [\alpha[f]\text{\_\_\_\_}] / \begin{bmatrix} +\text{\_\_\_\_NP} \\ \alpha\text{\_\_\_\_}[f] \end{bmatrix}$

This redundancy rule is of course the lexical analog of the transformational rule known as NP-Preposing or the inverse rule known as NP-Postposing. By accepting the lexical approach to participles outlined in section 2, we are thereby forced to choose the lexicalist model depicted in (62).

There is further evidence that this conclusion is not only desirable, but that it allows us to express a much deeper generalization. Note first that adjectives in *-able* which are derived from verbs exhibit one characteristic feature of passives. When the V of the adjective sequence selects NP as object, the related adjective itself selects this NP as subject. Chomsky noted this redundancy and proposed a lexical approach,

> insofar as a subregularity exists regarding selectional rules in the case of *-able*, it can be formulated as a lexical rule that assigns the feature [X____] to a lexical item [V-*able*] where V has the intrinsic selectional feature [____X].   [14: 56]

---

[12] Details concerning Aux and other material are omitted here. See [4]. Also note that Extraposition can be replaced with a redundancy rule so as to relate $\bar{\bar{S}}$ and $\bar{S}$ complements discussed in section 3 to a given predicate such as *surprise NP, be possible*, etc.

Chomsky's rule has been formulated by Hust [20: 67] as approximately the following[13]:

$$(64) \quad [+\underline{\quad}\#able] \longrightarrow [\alpha[f]\underline{\quad}] \; / \begin{bmatrix} +\underline{\quad\quad}NP \\ \alpha\underline{\quad\quad}[f] \end{bmatrix}$$

Hust has gone on to show that unpassive adjectives exhibit identical selectional properties. Thus, he was able to express the two sets of co-occurrence restriction by one general rule, repeated here as (65).

$$(65) \quad \begin{Bmatrix} [+\underline{\quad}\#able] \\ [+un\#\underline{\quad}\#ed] \end{Bmatrix} \longrightarrow [\alpha[f]\underline{\quad}] \; / \begin{bmatrix} +\underline{\quad\quad}NP \\ \alpha\underline{\quad\quad}[f] \end{bmatrix}$$

Of relevance for the present discussion is the fact that rule (63) can now be collapsed with Hust's rule (65), thus expressing a deeper generalization.

$$(66) \quad \begin{Bmatrix} [+\bar{\bar{V}}] \\ [+\underline{\quad}\#able] \\ [+un\#\underline{\quad}\#ed] \end{Bmatrix} \longrightarrow [\alpha[f]\underline{\quad}] \; / \begin{bmatrix} +\underline{\quad\quad}NP \\ \alpha\underline{\quad\quad}[f] \end{bmatrix}$$

The fact that a deeper generalization is naturally expressed within the lexical framework provides some justification for favoring it, at least in the case of passives.

6. THE TRANSFORMATIONAL COMPONENT

If local transformations are to be replaced with lexical redundancy rules, one might ask what transformations remain. A rather natural answer to this question is embodied in the following constraint on the form of transformations:

Variable Constraint:
All transformations make essential use of unbounded variables.

Thus, rules such as Question Formation, Relative Clause Formation,

---

[13] By convention it is assumed that all features present in the context of redundancy rules employing alpha notation are relevant, including +____NP itself. That is, although +____NP appears in the context of (64), it also is covered by the alpha feature of the context matrix and thus +NP____ is associated with adjectives in *-able*, etc.

Topicalization, and the like, all of which make essential use of variables which are unbounded, are the remaining candidates for the transformational component. This result is natural when contrasted with the observations of the preceding sections. Thus, unlike local transformations, no single lexical item serves as the locus of the long distance rules. Hence, long distance rules could not in principle be expressed as lexical redundancy rules. By contrast, given the Variable Constraint as a constraint on the form of transformations, local transformations no longer qualify as transformational rules.

These conclusions may prove too strong and additional analyses with precise formulations of the rules in question are needed before a final determination can be made. For example, there are some root transformations such as Subject-Aux Inversion which do not qualify as transformations by the Variable Constraint. Perhaps it would not be pointless to consider the feasibility of base generating all relevant structures of a local character by elaborating the base, as was done in section 3 with respect to sentential subjects and extraposed S's.

There is furthermore a model of grammar which is also worthy of serious consideration. This model can be thought of as a hybrid of the two models depicted in (62) and is laid out in picture form in (67).

(67)   INVERSE LEXICAL MODEL

deep structures (= base structures of
                      lexical model)

                      inverse T's

| base rules |

→ surface structures

| lexicon |
| redundancy rules relating active– passive, etc. |

If the Variable Constraint can be maintained, then the inverse lexical model is appealing for the following reason. By treating long distance rules in an inverse fashion, we succeed in expressing a generalization which cannot be expressed in the standard theory, as argued in Brame [2]. To see this, consider the following ungrammatical strings:

(68) a. *John saw the boy (who) Mary likes the girl.
     b. *What did they see the parade?
     c. *It was the car that I parked the truck in the garage.
     d. *Harry I saw Sue yesterday.
     e. *That she would do such a thing I believe Harry to be impossible.
     f. *They said she was examined by Dr. Qu, and examined by Dr. Qu she was arrested by the police.

Against the examples in (68), the following grammatical sentences should be contrasted.

(69) a. John saw the boy (who) Mary likes.
     b. What did they see?
     c. It was the car that I parked in the garage.
     d. Harry I saw yesterday.
     e. That she would do such a thing I believe to be impossible.
     f. They said she was examined by Dr. Qu, and examined by Dr. Qu she was.

Now how does the standard theory rule out the examples in (68)? According to Chomsky [13], (68a) is ruled out by the filtering function of transformations. Thus, special boundary symbols suffice to ensure identity in relative clauses and if the boundary symbol is not erased by application of Relative Clause Formation, which itself requires identity, then the internal occurrence of the boundary symbols will be sensitive to a filtering device, thus blocking the example. However, other examples in (68) will be ruled out by different mechanisms. Thus, (68b) will be blocked by virtue of the fact that *what* originates as the object of the verb *see*, which does not allow two objects. Hence by purely lexical considerations, (68b) is ruled out, as are some of the other examples in (68). But this surely constitutes a loss of generalization. An adequate theory would rule out all of (68) by the same basic mechanism. If we generate the examples in (69) directly, that is, if the *who* in (69a) is generated in Comp position, *what* in Comp position in (69b), *the car* in focus position in (69c), *Harry* in the topicalization position in (69d), etc., then it is possible to rule out all of (68) by purely lexical considerations, as advocated in [2].

REFERENCES

1. Akmajian, A., and Wasow, T. 1975. The constituent structure of VP and Aux and the position of the verb *be*. *Linguistic Analysis* 1: 205–45.
2. Brame, M. K. 1976. *Conjectures and Refutations in Syntax and Semantics*. New York: Elsevier North-Holland.
3. ———. 1977. Alternatives to the Tensed-S and Specified Subject Conditions. *Linguistics and Philosophy* 1.
4. ———. Forthcoming. *Base Generated Syntax*.
5. Bresnan, J. W. 1970. On complementizers: toward a syntactic theory of complement types. *Foundations of Language* 6: 297–321.
6. ———. 1971. Sentence stress and syntactic transformations. *Language* 47: 257–81.
7. ———. 1972. Theory of complementation in English syntax. Doctoral dissertation, MIT.
8. ———. 1973. Syntax of the comparative clause construction in English. *Linguistic Inquiry* 4: 275–343.
9. ———. 1977. Toward a realistic model of transformational grammar. Paper presented at the Bell Telephone Convocation at MIT.
10. Chomsky, N. 1975. *The Logical Structure of Linguistic Theory*. Plenum Press, New York. (Condensation of 1955 manuscript.)
11. ———. 1957. *Syntactic Structures*. The Hague: Mouton.
12. ———. 1964. *Current Issues in Linguistic Theory*. The Hague: Mouton.
13. ———. 1965. *Aspects of the Theory of Syntax*. Cambridge, Mass.: MIT Press.
14. ———. 1970. Remarks on nominalization. In *Readings in English Transformational Grammar*, R. A. Jacobs and P. S. Rosenbaum, eds. Waltham, Mass.: Ginn. Page references to reprinted version in *Studies on Semantics in Generative Grammar*, N. Chomsky, The Hague: Mouton.
15. Emonds, J. E. 1970. Root and structure-preserving transformations. Doctoral dissertation, MIT.
16. ———. 1972. A reformulation of certain syntactic transformations. In *Goals of Linguistic Theory*, S. Peters, ed. Englewood Cliffs, N. J.: Prentice-Hall.
17. ———. 1973. Alternatives to global constraints. *Glossa* 7: 39–62.
18. ———. 1976. *A Transformational Approach to English Syntax*. New York: Academic Press.
19. Higgins, F. R. 1973. On J. Emonds's analysis of extraposition. In *Syntax and Semantics* 2, J. P. Kimball, ed. New York: Seminar Press.
20. Horn, G. M. 1975. On the nonsentential nature of the POSS-ING construction in English. *Linguistic Analysis* 1: 333–87.
21. Hust, J. R. 1976. A lexical approach to the unpassive construction in English. Doctoral dissertation, University of Washington, Seattle.
22. ———. 1977. Lexical redundancy rules and the unpassive construction. *Linguistic Analysis* 3: 137–76.

23. Iwakura, K. 1977. The Auxiliary System in English. *Linguistic Analysis* 3: 101-36.
24. ———. 1977. The syntax of complement sentences in English. *Linguistic Analysis* 3: 000-00.
25. Jenkins, L. 1972. Modality in English syntax. Doctoral dissertation, MIT.
26. Klima, E. S. 1964. Negation in English. In *The Structure of Language: Readings in the Philosophy of Language*, J. A. Fodor and J. J. Katz, eds. Englewood Cliffs, N. J.: Prentice-Hall.
27. Kuno, S. 1973. Constraints on internal clauses and sentential subjects. *Linguistic Inquiry* 4: 363-85.
28. Lakoff, G. 1970. *Irregularity in Syntax*. New York: Holt, Rinehart and Winston.
29. Lakoff, R. T. 1969. Some reasons why there can't be any *some-any* rule. *Language* 45: 608-15.
30. Lasnik, H. and Fiengo, R. 1974. Complement object deletion. *Linguistic Inquiry* 5: 535-71.
31. Milsark, G. 1972. Re: Doubl-ing. *Linguistic Inquiry* 3: 542-49.
32. ———. 1977. Toward an explanation of certain peculiarities of the existential construction in English. *Linguistic Analysis* 3: 1-29.
33. Pullum, G. K. 1974. Restating Doubl-ing. *Glossa* 8: 109-20.
34. Rosenbaum, P. S. 1967. *The Grammar of English Predicate Complement Constructions*. Cambridge, Mass.: MIT Press.
35. Ross, J. R. 1967. Constraints on variables in syntax. Doctoral dissertation, MIT.
36. ———. 1972. Doubl-ing. *Linguistic Inquiry* 3: 61-86.
37. Seuren, P. A. M., ed. 1974. *Semantic Syntax*. London: Oxford University Press.

ALTERNATIVES TO THE TENSED S AND SPECIFIED SUBJECT CONDITIONS

Sensei, why do we lose the right wing interpretation?

It is not good for Communists to work in defense plants.
Defense plants are not good for Communists to work in.

Don't let them fool you, gakusei! It's really a matter of interpretation, not movement.

0. General Introduction

1. Introduction to TSC and SSC

2. Motivation for SSC and TSC: A Critique
   2.1 Object Shift
   2.2 *each*-Movement and TSC
   2.3 *each*-Movement and SSC
   2.4 Unlike Person Constraint and Disjoint Reference
   2.5 *Wh*-Movement
   2.6 Scope of Negation
   2.7 Passive
   2.8 Naturalness

3. Counterexamples to SSC, TSC, and Subjacency
   3.1 Introduction to Subjacency and Successive Cyclicity
   3.2 Counterexamples
       3.2.1 Clefting
       3.2.2 Comparative Subdeletion
       3.2.3 *wh*-Movement
       3.2.4 *each*-Movement
       3.2.5 Object Shift
       3.2.6 Superiority

4. Conclusion

   Notes

   References

ALTERNATIVES TO THE TENSED S AND SPECIFIED SUBJECT CONDITIONS*

0. GENERAL INTRODUCTION

In his contribution to the Halle Festschrift, Chomsky provides a battery of arguments for his Specified Subject and Tensed S Conditions. Chomsky argues that these conditions provide a unified account of a wide range of disparate facts. More recently, this earlier work has led to the development of trace theory, with the accompanying claim that all aspects of semantic interpretation are determined by surface structure.[1] It is my opinion that this kind of enterprise – a detailed discussion of a wide range of data, together with an explicit theory advanced to explain the data – is precisely the kind of enterprise that linguists must undertake if advances are to be made in syntax and neighboring disciplines. For only when commitments are made to detailed analyses is the productive potential of the critical method fully realized in the face of analyses and theories which do not reflect the true nature of things.

In the following pages I will undertake a critical reappraisal of the evidence advanced to support the arguments for the Specified Subject and Tensed S Conditions in Chomsky's original paper [12].[2] A careful look at the evidence has convinced me that there are plausible alternatives for dealing with the data provided as motivation for these conditions. In fact, it can be shown, I will argue, that to treat the data by means of these conditions leads in many instances to a loss of generalization; in other instances, the conditions approach raises more problems than it solves.

* A preliminary draft of this paper was written in the winter of 1975 and constituted the subject matter of a seminar given at the University of Washington during the fall of 1975.

183

After discussing and criticizing the Specified Subject and Tensed S Conditions, I will turn to a brief discussion and critique of Chomsky's Subjacency and Superiority Conditions. These too can be criticized with some force, I believe.

1. INTRODUCTION TO TSC AND SSC

Let us first consider SSC. This condition can be illustrated by considering the well-known rule of Object Shift (= Tough Movement). It is often claimed that this rule relates pairs such as the following.

(1) a.　It is not easy for a novice to faro a deck of cards.
　　b.　A deck of cards is not easy for a novice to faro.
(2) a.　It is hard to deal deceptive seconds without arousing suspicion.
　　b.　Deceptive seconds are hard to deal without arousing suspicion.

The traditional analysis has it that Object Shift moves the object of the complement, in these examples, *a deck of cards* in (1a) and *deceptive seconds* in (2a), and substitutes it for *it* in the matrix. Now a problem immediately arises in connection with (3a).

(3) a.　It is pleasant for the rich for poor immigrants to do the hard work.
　　b.　*The hard work is pleasant for the rich for poor immigrants to do.

The problem is why the object *the hard work* in (3a) cannot be shifted by Object Shift to yield (3b). According to Chomsky, movement is blocked in (3a) by a constraint on transformations. This constraint prohibits the movement, deletion, etc. of a category across a specified subject, where specified subject amounts to, roughly, a lexical subject (although the revised definition of specified subject will be discussed below). A simplified formulation of this constraint is given in (4).

(4)　　SSC: No rule can involve X, Y in the structure

$$\ldots X \ldots [_\alpha \ldots Z \ldots -WYV \ldots] \ldots$$

where Z is the specified subject of WYV in α, a cyclic category.

The effects of this constraint are illustrated diagrammatically in (5).

(5) X   Z   Y
　　| | |
　　It is pleasant for the rich [$_S$ for poor immigrants to do the hard work]
　　↑_____×_____|

Since *the poor immigrants* functions as a specified subject, *the hard work* cannot cross to substitute for *it*.

Let us now turn to additional examples illustrating a prohibition against Object Shift.

(6) a.   It is good that C. C. Wei invented the precision bidding system.

    b.   *The precision bidding system is good that C. C. Wei invented.

Again we see that Object Shift cannot apply to (6a) to give (6b). The prohibition of course follows from SSC, but there is a second condition which also serves to block (6b). This condition prohibits movement or deletion from a tensed sentence and is repeated in a somewhat simplified form as (7).

(7)   TSC: No rule can involve X, Y in the structure

$$\ldots X \ldots [_{\alpha} \ldots Y \ldots] \ldots$$

where α is a tensed sentence.

Since the embedded complement of (6a) is a tensed sentence, by TSC it is not possible to extract *the precision bidding system* by Object Shift.[3]

2. MOTIVATION FOR SSC AND TSC: A CRITIQUE

In this section I will examine Chomsky's motivation for SSC and TSC and provide plausible alternatives to account for the relevant range of data. I will show that these alternatives are independently justified inasmuch as they account for facts which are not treated by SSC and TSC. Thus, it appears that these conditions may be artifacts.

2.1 *Object Shift*

Since SSC and TSC have been introduced by way of Object Shift in section 1, let us now consider an alternative and historically antecedent account of the relevant range of data. In [7] Bresnan made the following observation.

It has been proposed ... by Lees 1960 ... that certain infinitival complements should be derived from deep-structure VP's rather than S's. Suppose this proposal is applied to the analysis of certain adjective plus complement constructions. [7:263]

According to Bresnan's proposal, following Lees, some adjectives, such as *obvious, clear*, etc. are lexically subcategorized to select S's, but not VP's, while others, such as *tough* are subcategorized to select VP's or PP + VP but not S's. This situation is illustrated in (8).

(8) a.   It is obvious [s that Mahler composed that symphony]

    b.   It will be tough [PP for some students][VP to solve that problem]

Bresnan provides a wealth of evidence to show that predicates such as *tough* should not be analyzed as selecting an S complement. Here I will repeat only one of those arguments.

Several facts argue against the sentential analysis: first, if there were an underlying sentence, one would normally expect a sentence-cyclic transformation such as *There*-Insertion to take place. But though one can say *It will be tough for at least some students to be in class on time*, one cannot say *It will be tough for there to be at least some students in class on time*. [7:264]

Bresnan contrasts this situation with predicates such as *eager* which do select S complements and consequently do permit *There*-Insertion: *The administration is eager for there to be at least some students in class on time.*

Now, in connection with (8), the crucial observation is that Object Shift correlates with presence of VP or PP + VP complement and is not allowed in the case of S or PP + S complement.

(9) a.   *That symphony is obvious that Mahler composed.

  b.   That problem will be tough for some students to solve.

The obvious conclusion is that Object Shift does not apply to S complements. In other words, the rule of Object Shift should be formulated so as to be sensitive to VP or PP + VP complements. Bresnan's tentative formulation along these lines is given in (10).[4]

(10)   Object Shift: $[_S \Delta$ Pred (PP) $[_{VP}$ V* (P) NP]]

This analysis provides an immediate explanation for the ungrammaticality of Chomsky's (3b) and for example (6) cited above in section 1.

(11) a.   *The hard work is pleasant for the rich $[_S$ for poor immigrants to do]

  b.   *The precision bidding system is good $[_S$ that C. C. Wei invented]

The explicit formulation of Object Shift as (10) does not allow extraction of an NP from an S complement. Therefore (11a) and (11b) cannot be generated. Thus, SSC and TSC are not supported by movement under Object Shift.

This discussion highlights a rather important point relating to all syntactic research, namely, that serious discussion can ensue only when explicit formulations of the rules in question are provided. In this case Bresnan's formulation leads to a solution for an outstanding puzzle. The puzzle involves certain ambiguous constructions noticed by traditional grammarians such as Jespersen and later by Lees.

There is in fact a class of adjectives permitting both S and PP + VP complements – namely, the class including *good, bad, sweet, pleasant,* and *appropriate*; the ambiguity in such cases is noted by Lees. The sentence *It is good for John to leave* may mean either 'For John to leave is good = It is good (for John to leave)' or 'To leave is good for John = It is good for John (to leave.)' Lees maintains a clear distinction between the ambiguous class (*good*; his type 7) and the unambiguous class (*hard, tough*; his type 8). [7:266–7].

Now the puzzle is this: whereas (12a) is ambiguous, the result of applying Object Shift in (12b) is not ambiguous.

(12) a. It is good for John to learn such things.
     b. Such things are good for John to learn.

Example (12b) receives the interpretation 'To learn such things is good for John' but not 'For John to learn such things is good'. What is the explanation for the absence of ambiguity under transformation? Obviously Bresnan's rule of Object Shift predicts that the object NP *such things* will be shifted from the VP complement only. Therefore, it follows that (12b) will receive the PP + VP interpretation and not the S interpretation for the complement structure. This is accomplished without theoretical elaboration. Let us consider briefly how Chomsky's constraints would express these facts.

First, consider example (9b). According to Chomsky, the underlying representation is roughly (13).

(13)   It will be tough [$_{PP}$ for some students] [$_S$ for PRO to solve that problem]

Chomsky attempts to preserve the abstract S by postulating an abstract subject PRO. This PRO is taken to be an unspecified subject, and therefore SSC will not block Object Shift, which allows extraction of an NP from S provided SSC and TSC are not violated. Now, turning to (12), Chomsky would propose two underlying sources for (12a) corresponding to the two interpretations.

(14) a. It is good [$_S$ for John to learn such things]
     b. It is good [$_{PP}$ for John] [$_S$ for PRO to learn such things]

In the case of (14a) Object Shift will be inapplicable because of SSC. However, Object Shift will apply to (14b), just as in (13), yielding (12b). Thus, by recourse to SSC, Chomsky is also able to predict the nonambiguity of (12b).

In comparing the two alternatives it is important to bear in mind that Bresnan does not employ ad hoc extensions (of what we agree appears on the surface) such as the abstract S and PRO. Now such extensions are not objectionable in themselves, but if no independent motivation can be given to support them, the theory which avoids such elaborations is to be favored. In this case, no evidence is offered to support the abstract S or the PRO. In fact, it would appear that new problems entailing further ad hoc excesses are a consequence of the proposed elaborations.

Notice first that preservation of the abstract S creates a gap in phrase structure as well as in the lexicon in terms of lexical subcategorization. Thus, if all VP-like complements are derived from S complements, there will be no VP complements expressed in the phrase structure rules or in lexical subcatorization. But certainly one expects to find VP complements, since one finds all the other major categories such as S, NP, and AP. This gap is closed if VP complements are in fact VP's in underlying representations. Second, notice that the availability of PRO now raises the question of distributional generality. Since true NP's can occupy all the NP positions provided by the phrase structure rules, e.g. the object position, object of preposition position, subject position, etc., one would expect PRO, if it really exists, to occupy the full range of NP positions provided by the phrase structure rules. But no evidence has been advanced to indicate that PRO occupies anything but the subject position. Surely this limited distribution should lead us to question the existence of PRO. Third, the availability of the abstract S raises problems of the following sort. How are we to block underlying complement structures from being associated with *tough* when they are of the following type?

(15) a.   It is tough [s for John to learn such things]
     b.   It is tough [s for us to yield to such demands]

According to Lees and Bresnan, adjectives such as *tough* do not select S complements, but rather only PP + VP or VP complements. And this claim is borne out, at least for me, by the fact that *It is tough for John to learn such things* cannot receive an interpretation 'For John to lean such things is tough' but rather must be interpreted as 'To learn such things is tough for John' and likewise for (15b). Notice that it will not do to block (15) by simply marking *tough* to obligatorily select a PP, i.e. a PP + S complement. This is so in view of examples such as (16).

(16)   It is tough to solve such problems.

If (16) derives from *It is tough* [s *for PRO to solve such problems*], then one should expect (15) to be a legitimate structure; but it is not, at least for speakers such as Lees, Bresnan, and myself. On the other hand, if (16) derives from a source such as *It is tough* [pp *for PRO*] [s *for PRO to solve such problems*], then new difficulties arise. First, a new rule will have to be postulated to delete the PP *for PRO*. This rule is postulated for no other reason than to undo the results the abstractions entail and in this sense is ad hoc. Second, what now is to block *It is tough for PRO* [*for John to solve such problems*]? This in turn raises the general problem of how the presence of PRO in the abstract S subject position is to be insured when PP is present. Thus, what is to block *It is tough for John* [s *for Mary to leave*]?

It is certainly remarkable that none of the problems even arise within the VP framework. All other things being equal, I think the conclusion is inescapable. The VP framework is to be favored over the analysis adopting the abstract S, PRO, and constraints such as SSC and TSC. Until the problems raised here can be satisfactorily resolved and independent justification provided for the theoretical elaborations entailed by the framework adopted by Chomsky, Object Shift phenomena cannot be taken as evidence for SSC and TSC.[5]

2.2. Each-*Movement and TSC*

Chomsky [12] claims to follow Dougherty [16] in assuming a rule which moves *each* so as to relate pairs such as the following.[6]

(17) a.   The candidates each hated the other.
     b.   The candidates hated each other.

Chomsky calls this rule *each*-Movement (and occasionally *each*-Insertion [12:239]) and he draws on it throughout his study as evidence to support SSC and TSC. Thus, consider the difference between (18) and (19).

(18) a.   The candidates each expected the other to win.
     b.   The candidates expected each other to win.
(19) a.   The candidates each expected that the other would win.
     b.   *The candidates expected that each other would win.

It is claimed that (18b) derives from (18a) via *each*-Movement (hereafter EM), whereas (19b) does not derive from (19a) by virtue of the fact that EM is blocked by TSC as illustrated in (20).

(20)

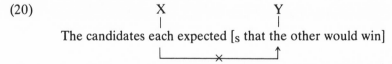

Since *that the other would win* is a tensed sentence, application of EM to (19a) would constitute a violation of TSC. EM is not prohibited from applying to (18a), however, since *the other to win* is not a tensed sentence.

Now it can be shown that EM is not a movement rule. Rather, *each other* should be generated as such in the base.[7] The question therefore shifts from that of explaining why EM cannot apply to (19a) to that of why *each other* cannot be generated directly in (19b), or, alternatively, why (19b) is filtered in the event that it is generated. Chomsky recognizes the latter possibility when he remarks: "Notice that if one were to accept the alternative analysis of Jackendoff (1969), principle (20) [= TSC, MKB] would again apply – in this case, not to a movement rule but to a rule of interpretation" [12:238, fn. 17]. Thus, again we see that TSC is instrumental in accounting for the deviance of (19b).

There is some reason to believe, however, that TSC has nothing to do with the deviance of (19b). Consider by way of example the following cases.

(21) a. *Each other will win.
     b. *The boys and each other will win.

The point is simply this. Under the conditions approach, TSC is invoked in ruling out (19b), whereas it plays no role whatsoever in ruling out (21a) and (21b). But, clearly, the mechanism that is independently needed to rule out (21a) and (21b) can be utilized to rule out (19b), in which case (19b) cannot be said to constitute motivation for TSC. We might do this by constraining lexical insertion so that only subject pronouns are inserted into the subject position of tensed S's. Reciprocals such as *each other*, being object pronouns, would not be inserted into the subject position, as desired. Formally, this might be accomplished by enriching the phrase structure rules or by expanding the complex symbol associated with Pronoun to yield [−objective] when followed by Aux. Subject pronouns would then be marked with this feature, as opposed to objective pronouns such as *each other, himself, him,* etc., which are [+objective]. Such an account would insure that *each other* could not be inserted into the subject position of (21a), (21b), and also (19b). This proposal, incidentally, is simply a lexical analogue of Klima's case marking rule, which marks the subject of a tensed S as nominative. Such an account immediately generalizes to account for the following data.

(22) a. *Himself will win.
     b. *Him will win.
     c. He will win.

It will automatically allow for the following distinctions.

(23) a. *We believe that each other are incorrect.
     b. We believe that each other's theories are incorrect.

It also provides for the following distribution of data.

(24) a. The candidates knew that pictures of each other would be on sale.
     b. The candidates knew that pictures of themselves would be on sale.
     c. The candidates knew that pictures of them would be on sale.

The constraint against the appearance of *each other* in the subject position of a tensed S is thus seen to be a special case of a more general lexical or base rule constraint against object pronouns in this position. TSC is incapable in principle of accounting for this range of data. Rather, it appears to lead to a loss of generalization in this area.

There is a further consideration which is worthy of comment. This concerns languages with an underlying order of constituents which differs from the English SVO order. Joan Bresnan has informed me that my idea that *each other* and other instances of 'bound anaphora' must agree with their subjects predicts that reciprocals and reflexives could precede their antecedents in VOS languages, whereas Chomsky's assumption that bound anaphors agree with arbitrary antecedents, subject to SSC and conditions on *proper binding*, predicts that this could happen only if NP-movements are subject to the same conditions, namely rightward movement as opposed to leftward. If reciprocals and reflexives in Malgasy are bound anaphora, Bresnan points out that such a language would appear to support my assumption and disconfirm Chomsky's, because reflexives do precede their subjects, whereas NP-movements are leftward.

Now let us turn to the following examples.

(25) a. The boys each think that Bill will fool the other.
  b. *The boys think that Bill will fool each other.
(26) a. Bill thinks that the boys each will fool the other.
  b. Bill thinks that the boys will fool each other.

Under the movement approach to *each other*, (25b) cannot derive from (25a) because of TSC, whereas (26b) can derive from (26a) without incident. But, as noted above, the movement approach is misguided.[8] Therefore, according to Chomsky's interpretive analogue, *each other* and *the boys* in (25b) cannot be related by the interpretive anaphora rule because of TSC (and also by virtue of SSC).

But TSC again has nothing to do with the deviance of (25b). To see this consider the following examples.

(27) a. *Bill will fool each other.
  b. The boys will fool each other.

The most obvious and straightforward account of (27a) is simply that *each other* and Bill are anaphoric, but since anaphorically related NP's must agree in number and gender, (27a) constitutes a violation of concord, *Bill* being singular and *each other* plural. Such an account generalizes to other anaphoric pronouns.

(28) a. *Bill likes herself.
     b. *Bill likes themselves.

This account also generalizes to rule out (25b), granted that anaphoric pronouns such as *each other* are marked as anaphoric with their subject antecedents.

   In summary, there are two assumptions. First, I assume a rule of anaphora which marks anaphoric pronouns such as reciprocals and reflexives as anaphoric to their subject antecedents.[9] Let us write this interpreted relation as (NP_i, NP_j), to be read *NP_i is anaphoric to NP_j*, where NP_i is an anaphoric pronoun and NP_j is its subject antecedent. Second, I assume that there is a filter which marks those sentences in which the anaphorically related NP's differ in concord as ill-formed. Such a filter might be formulated in the following way.

(29)   Gender/Number Filter:
         $[_s \ldots NP_i \ldots NP_j \ldots] \rightarrow \#$
         $\quad\quad\,\alpha F \quad\; -\alpha F$
         where (NP_j, NP_i) and F is gender or number

Now it is true that the interpretive rule which provides us with the anaphoric relations (NP_i, NP_j) must itself be constrained so that it does not apply across tensed S's; however, it is shown in [6] that TSC receives no support from the general rule of anaphora.

   The point is again this. Even Chomsky must develop an independent mechanism for marking examples such as (27a) and (28) as deviant. But this independently needed mechanism, which I have formulated as (29), should in fact be utilized to account for the deviance of (25b). Once this independent device is brought to bear, examples such as (25b) cease to count as evidence for TSC.

2.3. *EM and SSC*

On quite analogous grounds it can be shown that EM does not constitute evidence for SSC. Consider the argument for SSC based on the following examples.

(30) a. The men each expect Bill to see the other.
     b. *The men expect Bill to see each other.

According to the conditions approach, EM is blocked by SSC from applying to (30a) to yield (30b). Or, looking at it from the interpretive perspective, *each other* cannot be marked as anaphoric to *the men* in (30b) because of SSC, as illustrated below.

(31)

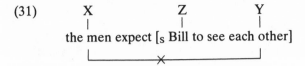

However, here, as in the case of (25b), special conditions such as SSC are superfluous. Completely independent mechanisms such as the rule of anaphora will mark *Bill* and *each other* as standing in an anaphoric relationship, i.e. (*each other, Bill*), since *Bill* is the antecedent subject. This in turn constitutes a violation of number agreement, so that (30b) is filtered by (29). This explanation derives additional support from the fact that the following must be filtered in a completely analogous fashion.

(32) a. *John's pictures of each other are on the table.
     b. *John's pictures of themselves are on the table.
     c. *The men's pictures of himself are on the table.
     d. *John's pictures of one another are on the table.

On the other hand, the following examples are not filtered by (29).

(33) a. The men's pictures of each other are on the table.
     b. John's pictures of himself are on the table.
     c. The men's pictures of one another are on the table.

In (32) the subject and anaphoric pronoun must again stand in an anaphoric relationship, but this time the relevant phrase is the cyclic category NP as opposed to S. These anaphoric relations, however, give rise to concord violations. Quite apart from SSC, some extra mechanism is required to mark the examples of (32) as deviant. The claim made here is that precisely this mechanism should constitute the explanation for the deviance of (30b). This conclusion shows that SSC derives no support from examples such as (30b).

2.4. *Unlike Person Constraint and Disjoint Reference*

Chomsky adduces the following examples with associated grammaticality judgments.

(34) a. *I saw me.
     b. *I watched us leaving.
     c. *We watched me leaving.
     d. *You (all) noticed you standing there.

Following Postal, Chomsky claims

> ... the point seems to be that a rule of interpretation RI applying to the structure NP–V–NP (among others) seeks to interpret the two NPs as nonintersecting in reference, and where this is impossible (as in the case of first and second person pronouns . . .), it assigns 'strangeness', marking the sentence with *. [12:241]

Chomsky goes on to cite the following examples.

(35) a.   *We* expect them to visit *me*; *I* expect them to visit *us* (*me*).
   b.   *We expect *me* to visit them; *I expect *us* (*me*) to visit them.
   c.   *We expect *me* to be visited by them; *I expect *us* (*me*) to be visited by them.
   d.   *We* believe *I* may still win; *I* believe *we* (*I*) may still win.

In connection with (35a) and (35d), it is claimed that SSC and TSC block RI, and thus these examples are not starred. "Therefore in these sentences the pair of italicized NPs may intersect in reference; the sentences are not marked with * by RI" [12:241].

Let us attempt to be more explicit about what is asserted in the foregoing quote. First, the reference sets denoted by NPs are interpreted as non-intersecting, i.e. their intersection is null, when SSC and TSC do not function to block this interpretation. This claim is represented by the following rule, where Ref (X) indicates the reference set denoted by X.[10]

(36) RI_1: $Ref(NP_i) \cap Ref(NP_j) = \phi$ if $[_s \ldots NP_i \ldots NP_j \ldots]$

Second, some sentences are actually starred when the NPs involved are both first person or both second person pronouns. This claim is represented by the following rule.

(37) RI_2: $[_s \ldots NP_i \ldots NP_j \ldots] \rightarrow *$
        where NP_i and NP_j are both first or second person pronouns

Now there is some reason to suspect that reference, intersecting or otherwise, is not crucial to this discussion. First of all, note that (35b) and (35c) are in fact perfectly grammatical. This fact could be accounted for by incorporating a further restriction into (37), namely, that NP_i and NP_j agree in number as well as person (exclusive of third person). However, there is another fact, and this is simply that (34a–d) are also perfectly grammatical in spite of the claim to the contrary. What is remarkable about (34a), for example, is not that it is ungrammatical, but, rather, that it receives a special interpretation, which, to borrow a term from Lewis, we might call the *counterpart* interpretation. To see that such examples are indeed grammatical, we might consider examples involving more contextual material, such as the examples listed under (38).

(38) a.   While watching TV the other day, I saw (us, me) leaving.

b.   Why don't you come up to my place and we'll watch (us, me) leaving on TV.

c.   If I were you, I would kiss me.

d.   I dreamed I was you and that I kissed me.

Now the crucial point here is not that rules such as (36) and (37) are blocked by conditions such as SSC and TSC, but rather that certain pronouns are interpreted as counterparts under structural conditions which turn out to be quite analogous to those required for anaphora. Thus, again representing the anaphora relation with parentheses as in section 2.2 and representing the counterpart relation with angled brackets, we observe the following.

(39) a.	I saw myself	(myself, I)
b.	I saw me.	⟨me, I⟩
(40) a.	I know you saw myself.	~ (myself, I)
b.	I know you saw me.	~ ⟨me, I⟩
(41) a.	I told myself to leave.	(myself, I)
b.	I told me to leave.	⟨me, I⟩
(42) a.	I told you to kiss myself.	~ (myself, I)
b.	I told you to kiss me.	~ ⟨me, I⟩

This parallelism is expressed in a general way in the theory outlined in [6], where counterpart interpretation, like anaphora, is an interpreted syntactic relation. Though coreference must take such syntactic relations into account, neither anaphora nor counterpart itself can be considered a semantic relation on a par with pronominalization.[11] In conclusion, the relevant examples cannot be considered as evidence for SSC or TSC.

There is, incidentally, evidence of another sort, brought to my attention by Joan Bresnan, which suggests that intersecting reference is not crucial to the correct account of the relevant examples. Thus, consider the following examples.

(43) a.   *John and Bill* like *him*.

b.   *John and Bill* like *them*.

Now *him* in (43a) and *them* in (43b), under the approach being criticized here, exhibit reference sets which do not intersect with the reference of *John and Bill*, which is presumably the set of John and Bill. But if reference is indeed involved, then an NP denoting the complement set of John and Bill should allow pronominal reference to John and Bill. However, this prediction is not borne out in the relevant examples listed in (44).

(44) a.   *Neither John nor Bill* like *him*.

b.   *Neither John nor Bill* like *them*.

In (44), just as in (43), the reference of *him* and *them* cannot intersect with the set denoted by the subject, the set of John and Bill in the case of (43) and the complement set in the case of (44). This suggests that it is not reference, but rather the counterpart relation that we are dealing with here since in both (43) and (44) the pronouns can be interpreted as counterparts to their subjects. This conclusion is supported by the fact that reflexive pronouns are also possible under analogous conditions.

(45) a.   John and Bill like themselves.
     b.   Neither John nor Bill like themselves (likes himself).

The correlation between anaphora and counterpart is thus seen to hold in these cases as well. This shows that such relations are syntactic and do not depend on reference, in spite of the fact that any theory of reference will take such relations into account.

2.5 Wh-*Movement*

The following examples are offered as further motivation for SSC.

(46) a.   Who did you see pictures of?
     b.   *Who did you see John's pictures of?

In (46b) *John's* is a specified subject, whereas (46a) has no subject associated with *pictures*.[12] Thus, it is argued, (35b) constitutes a violation of SSC, accounting for its deviance.

Some speakers have disagreed with the grammaticality judgments indicated in (46), maintaining that (46b) is perfectly grammatical. Since (46a) and (46b) are quite similar structurally (they do differ, as will be noted below), it seems reasonable that some speakers will provide a parsing of (46b) on analogy with (46a). This false parsing should be due to performance factors and can be dismissed in view of many additional clear-cut examples, including the following.

(47) a.   Bill saw paintings by a famous artist.
     b.   Which artist did Bill see paintings by?
(48) a.   Bill saw Mary's paintings by a famous artist.
     b.   *Which artist did Bill see Mary's paintings by?

However, additional examples show that it is not a fact about subjects, i.e. SSC, that accounts for the deviance of (46b) and (48b).

(49) a.   Bill saw those paintings by Rembrandt.
     b.   *Which artist did Bill see those paintings by?
(50) a.   Mary saw those pictures of Harry.
     b.   *Who did Mary see those pictures of?

Chomsky recognizes that determiners like *those, these, the*, etc. lead to violations and suggests that SSC might be refined to accommodate "the feature [+definite] as well as the property of lexical specification" [12:239, fn. 19]. He goes on to consider accounting for "a three-way gradation of acceptability" with examples such as (46b) apparently being less acceptable that (49b) and (50b). Although there may indeed be recognizable degrees of acceptability in these examples, it seems that these acceptability judgments ought to be construed as a relatively clear case of a performance phenomenon. Most speakers, would react even more strongly against (51), for example, than (46b) because the subject is even more complex.

(51)   *Who did Bill see John and Mary's pictures of?

It seems better to assume that all such example are ungrammatical, their deviance being due not to the presence of subjects, but rather to the presence of constructions bearing heads. I have in mind here a structural difference between *pictures of NP* on the one hand and *Det pictures of NP* on the other, where Det may dominate articles or possessive NPs. One proposal for such a distinction is provided in (52).

(52) a. $[_{\bar{N}}$ pictures $[_{PP}$ of $N]_{PP}]_{\bar{N}}$
     b. $[_{\bar{\bar{N}}}$ Det $[_{\bar{N}}$ pictures $[_{PP}$ of $N]_{PP}]_{\bar{N}}]_{\bar{\bar{N}}}$

Given such a structural difference one might propose a general constraint on the scope of rules applying to structures such as (52b). In fact, such a constraint has been proposed by a number of authors. A recent formulation of the Head Constraint by van Riemsdijk [25] is the following.

(53)   Head Constraint:
        No rule may involve X and Y in the structure
        $\dots X \dots [_{H^n} \dots [_{H^1} \dots H \dots Y \dots]_{H^1} \dots]_{H^n} \dots$
        where H is the phonologically specified head and H^n is the
        maximal projection of H

The Head Constraint is an interesting alternative to SSC. Together with (52a, b), it correctly predicts that (46a) and (47b) are grammatical, while it predicts that (46b), (48b), (49b), and (50b) are not. Moreover, it does not block the following, given rational assumptions about the structure of such examples.

(54) a.   Who do you expect John to talk to?
     b.   Who do you want Bill to see?

Such examples as these are counterexamples to SSC and occasion new elaborations such as successive cyclicity with special COMP nodes. The Head Constraint does not entail these devices.

There is, however, evidence that the Head Constraint is not the correct account in such cases. Consider, for example, the important fact that the following examples exhibit a range of grammaticality completely analogous to the foregoing examples.[13]

(55) a. Who saw pictures of who(m)?
    b. *Who saw John's pictures of who(m)?
    c. *Who saw those pictures of who(m)?
(56) a. Who saw pictures by who(m)?
    b. *Who saw Mary's pictures by who(m)?
    c. *Who saw those pictures by who(m)?

Examples such as these should be read without echo intonation. They demonstrate, I believe, that the constraints approach to such phenomena is fundamentally misguided. Rather, the underlying structural difference laid out in (52) (or some such structural difference) should be crucial to filtering (or lexical insertion) of scope words such as *who, what*, etc. Such an account, elaborated in [6] and to some extent in the following subsection, does not make reference to SSC.

2.6. *Scope of Negation*

A further argument for SSC is attributed to Lasnik and is based on examples such as the following.

(57) a. I didn't see many of the pictures.
    b. I didn't see pictures of many of the children.
    c. I didn't see John's pictures of many of the children.

Chomsky claims that (57a) and (57b) are ambiguous. On one reading, the negative element can be associated with *many*; on the other reading, it is associated with *see*. On the former reading of (57a), few pictures were seen, while on the latter reading, many or few may have been seen, but many were not seen. A similar ambiguity is said to hold of (57b). However, it is claimed that (57c) is not ambiguous. It can bear only the interpretation associating the negative element with the verb *see*. The negative element cannot be associated with *many* in (57c). The reason for this is that SSC blocks interpretation across the specified subject *John's*.

These judgments are subtle and I find difficulty sorting out the various interpretations, but they are not implausible. However, if scope of negation can be used to argue for SSC and TSC, certainly it can be used to argue against SSC and TSC if relevant examples can be found. In fact, it is well known that negation in matrix structures can affect material in complement structures. Thus, to take a familiar example from Chomsky [11], we find the following facts concerning *until* phrases.

(58) a. *Bill will leave until midnight.
　　b. Bill will not leave until midnight.

Thus, *until midnight* must fall within the scope of negation in order for the sentence to exhibit full grammaticality. But now consider the fact that the following is fully grammatical.

(59)　Mary didn't expect Bill to leave until midnight.

Now, according to the approach being criticized here, *Bill* is a specified subject in (59), and yet the scope of negation is able to filter past *Bill* so as to permit the *until* phrase. Such examples provide strong counterevidence to SSC, and analogous examples can be multiplied. Thus, idioms such as *give a damn*, *cut any ice*, and others behave like the *until* phrase in exhibiting full grammaticality in the presence of negation.[14]

(60) a. *We give a damn whether we pass or fail.
　　　We don't give a damn whether we pass or fail.
　　b. *It cuts any ice whether you pass or fail.
　　　It doesn't cut any ice whether you pass or fail.

Again, the scope of negation is able to filter past the specified subject as exhibited in the following sentences.

(61) a. John doesn't expect us to give a damn whether we pass or fail.
　　b. John doesn't expect it to cut any ice whether you pass or fail.

Thus, the facts attributed to Lasnik do not support SSC.

Assuming that Lasnik's and Chomsky's judgments concerning the ambiguity of (57a, b) and the nonambiguity of (57c) are correct, it remains to provide an alternative explanation for these facts. In this connection let us note the following examples.

(62) a. I didn't see any of the children.
　　b. I didn't see pictures of any of the children.
　　c. *I didn't see John's pictures of any of the children.
(63) a. I didn't see any of the artists.
　　b. I didn't see pictures by any of the artists.
　　c. *I didn't see John's pictures by any of the artists.

These examples are quite analogous to those cited in (57), repeated here to bring out the parallelism.

(64) a. I didn't see many of the pictures.
     b. I didn't see pictures of many of the children.
     c. I didn't see John's pictures of many of the children.
(65) a. I didn't see many of the artists.
     b. I didn't see pictures by many of the artists.
     c. I didn't see John's pictures by many of the artists.

There is indeed an analogy here. *Many* may or may not receive negative scope, but in (64c) and (65c) it cannot, so these examples are unambiguous. *Any*, on the other hand, requires negative scope,[15] but does not have it in (62c) and (63c), so these sentences are deviant. Thus, there is a similarity, and the difference in grammaticality can be correlated with the following difference.

(66) a. *I saw any of the pictures.
     b. I saw many of the pictures.

That the generalization cuts deeper still can be seen by comparing (62)–(65) with the facts about reflexives to which we now return.

(67) a. The boys saw each other.
     b. The boys saw pictures of each other.
     c. *The boys saw John's pictures of each other.
(68) a. I saw myself.
     b. I saw pictures of myself.
     c. *I saw John's pictures of myself.

Clearly, SSC is the wrong way to go about generalizing the negation and anaphora cases. Further, the Head Constraint fails to generalize to the examples discussed in the previous subsection (repeated as (69)) which should be compared with (62)–(68).

(69) a. Who saw who(m)?
     b. Who saw pictures of who(m)?
     c. *Who saw John's pictures of who(m)?

Therefore, instead of approaching the problem negatively, i.e. by specifying what scope cannot do, let us approach the matter positively and stipulate what scope must do.

I have already suggested a means of attacking the facts about anaphora in subsection 2.2. It now remains to generalize such an account. In what follows I will sketch a general treatment for $\bar{\bar{N}}$; a more general account covering $\bar{S}$ as well can be found in [6].

Let us stipulate that scope items such as *who, what, any, ever*, etc. as well as anaphoric pronouns such as *each other, myself*, etc. be obligatorily related to their associated heads in the presence of $\bar{\bar{N}}$. This was the account provided for anaphoric relations earlier where it was assumed that *himself* is marked as anaphoric to *John* in (33b) and as anaphoric to *the men* in (32c). The latter example constitutes part of the motivation for a concord filter such as (29). Suppose now we do the same for the other scope phenomena. Pictorially, we might formulate the scope rule as follows.

(70)   Scope Rule: Interpret R(S, Det) in $[_{\bar{N}}H[\ldots S \ldots]]_{\bar{N}}$ where S is a scope word such as *wh, any, myself*, H is the lexical head of $\bar{\bar{N}}$, and R is the scope relation

A specific instance of the scope relation R is anaphora which was stated above as (NP_i, NP_j). Now in (62c) we get R *(any, John)*, but this does not satisfy the constraint that an affective item must be the second coordinate of R when *any* is the first coordinate. Therefore, (62c) is filtered in a way analogous to examples of concord disagreement in anaphora.

Within the framework I am advocating here, the key point is that scope items are obligatorily interpreted as related to their heads. Within the conditions framework, the affective contexts are blocked from having scope which crosses a head. My framework positively specifies its scope relations; the other allows arbitrary scope constrained by conditions such as SSC or the Head Constraint. In a sense, it says what cannot constitute a legitimate scope relation, rather than what can.

The theory advocated here should be able to express the following parallelism.

(71) a.   We believe that each other's theories are incorrect.
     b.   We don't believe that anyone's theories are incorrect.
(72) a.   *We believe that John's pictures of each other are on the table.
     b.   *We don't believe that John's pictures of anybody are on the table.
(73) a.   We believe that pictures of each other are on the table.
     b.   We don't believe that pictures of anybody are on the table.

Examples such as (71) are discussed in [6]. Here, let us be content to note that relative clauses exhibit a similar parallelism and are treated by the Scope Rule (70).

(74) a.   I saw *the boy who* hit *himself*
     b.   *I saw *the boy who* hit *myself*

(75) a. I never met *anyone who ever* won at baccarat.

      |_____|

  b. *I never met *the boy who ever* won at baccarat.

      |___×___|

(76) a. John is *the only boy who* saw *anything.*

      |_____|

  b. *John is *the boy who* saw *anything.*

      |_____×_____|

Notice that the relation is well-formed and hence is not filtered when there is no concord disagreement in the case of anaphora and when an affective element is present in the head in the case of a negative scope item such as *ever* or *anything.* Such an account can be generalized beyond $\bar{\bar{N}}$ as in [6]. This account correctly predicts the facts concerning scope of negation in (62) and (63), while allowing (59) and (61), which are counter examples to SSC.

2.7. *Passive*

Another argument offered as motivation for TSC concerns the following examples.

(77) a. I believe the dog is hungry.
    b. *The dog is believed is hungry by me.

According to Chomsky, there is no way to block the Passive transformation from applying to (77a) to yield the ungrammatical (77b) within the standard theory since nodes that dominate no terminal string play no role "in factoring terminal strings for transformation" [12:273, n55]. Thus, even though COMP intervenes between the verb *believe* and the NP *the dog* in the relevant deep structure (78), Passive will still apply.

(78)   I believe [$_s$ COMP the dog is hungry]

However, as Chomsky notes, "there are other conventions" that might be conceived, and one obvious proposal in this case is that nodes that dominate no terminal strings, such as COMP, do play a role in factoring terminal strings for transformation. If the rule of Passive is formulated so as to require that the object immediately follow the associated verb, then (77b) will be avoided under this alternative convention.

However, it seems to me that there is another even more plausible explanation for the ungrammaticality of (77b). This explanation rests on some results argued for in [3] and depends on base structures which are considerably less abstract than assumed in the standard theory. In [3] and [5] I argue that VP complements are generated directly, along with passives, expletive *there* sentences, raising sentences, etc. If this is the case, then it is necessary to explain why the following examples are ungrammatical.

(79) a. I persuaded Mary [$_{VP}$ is present]
    b. I expected Mary [$_{VP}$ is present]

One answer is to adopt Emonds' proposal that no Aux node be generated as an expansion of VP. Rather Aux is reserved for S and gives rise to *tense* (*M*). If Emonds' proposal is adopted, then (79a, b) cannot arise. Alternatively, Aux might be generated in the VP, but expanded only as *to* and possibly *ing* when dominated by VP. In either case, such restrictions on VP complements will allow both of the examples listed in (80) while prohibiting the examples in (81).

(80) a. Mary persuaded John to be quiet.
    b. John was persuaded by Mary to be quiet.
(81) a. *Mary persuaded John is quiet.
    b. *John was persuaded by Mary is quiet.

But clearly (81b) is analogous to (77b). Precisely the same restrictions on VP complements can be used to prohibit (77b) where *is hungry* is taken to be VP. Passive of course cannot apply to (77a) because it is not a transformation. Rather, passive structures are generated directly as argued in [3] and [5].

2.8. *Naturalness*

As a final argument for SSC, Chomsky notes that SSC "has a certain naturalness" in having "the effect of reducing ambiguity, or, to put it differently, of increasing the reliability of a reasonable perceptual strategy that seeks the nearest NP to a verb (or the head noun of a nominal phrase) as its subject" [12:270]. Thus, in the example *the men expected the police to arrest each other*, SSC reduces ambiguity by requiring the *each* of *each other* to be associated with *the police* and not the men. But, clearly, within the approach outlined in subsections 2.2, 2.3 and 2.6, this result is also obtained, and in a positive manner. Moreover, there is little to be gained by resorting to plausibility arguments based on very abstract ideas such as naturalness, given the poverty of our present understanding of what constitutes a natural syntactic process. Indeed languages are quite rampant with ambiguity and one might even argue that it is natural that languages are blessed with such richness. Whatever the case, naturalness is no substitute for internal arguments, and I do not see that naturalness provides any support for SSC over the alternatives sketched out here.

3. COUNTEREXAMPLES TO SSC, TSC, AND SUBJACENCY

I think that the foregoing discussion demonstrates that there is little motivation for SSC and TSC. Moreover, many of the facts brought to bear in section 2 argue against these conditions. In the present section I want to advance additional arguments against SSC, TSC, and a further condition, subjacency. Preparatory to presenting these arguments, let us review subjacency and its consequence, successive cyclicity.

3.1. *Introduction to Subjacency and Successive Cyclicity*

Chomsky notes examples such as those listed in (82).

(82) a. What did you tell me Bill saw?
     b. Who did you say left?

He points out that (82a) appears to violate both SSC and TSC, while (82b) appears to violate TSC. Therefore Chomsky reanalyses *wh*-fronting, utilizing Bresnan's COMP node, so as to move the *wh*-word leftward in a successive cyclic fashion as illustrated in (83).

(83) a. COMP you told me [s COMP Bill saw what]

     b. COMP you said [s COMP who left]

A more complicated example is (84a), which is derived in a successive cyclic fashion according to (84b).

(84) a. Who did John say that Bill wanted Harry to investigate?
     b.

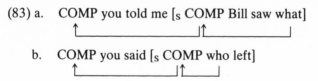

COMP John said [s COMP Bill wanted [s COMP Harry to investigate who]]

This analysis is apparently required given the new constraint Chomsky proposes.

(85)   Subjacency: No rule can affect material in two cyclic domains unless these domains are adjacent.

This condition has the effect of prohibiting *wh*-fronting in one sweep as in the traditional approach. Further, to avoid violations of TSC and SSC, these conditions are reformulated and collapsed to give the following.

(86)   No rule can involve X, Y in the structure
$\therefore$ X ... [$_\alpha$ ... Z ... $-$WYV ...] ...
where   (a) Z is the specified subject of WYV
or (b) Y is in COMP and X is not in COMP
or (c) Y is not in COMP and α is a tensed S

(86a) is SSC and (86c) is TSC revised so as to allow extraction when Y, in the above case the *wh*-NP, is in COMP. Condition (86b) prohibits movement from COMP unless the relevant trigger is itself in COMP. The net effect is that *wh*-fronting proceeds from COMP to COMP.

Before turning to the counterevidence, let us consider one further revision of SSC. This revision is occasioned by examples such as the following.

(87) a.   We each persuaded Bill to kill the other.
    b.   *We persuaded Bill to kill each other.

According to (86), EM (or the interpretive analogue) should not be blocked in (87a). Therefore (87b) should be grammatical. This follows from the fact that the embedded clause contains PRO in Chomsky's framework, which is an unspecified subject under the previous definition. To obtain the situation illustrated in (88), Chomsky revises SSC as in (89).

(88)   We each persuaded Bill [COMP PRO to kill the other]
         |_____×_____↑

(89)   SSC: No rule can involve, X, Y in the structure
... X ... [... Z ... $-$WYV ...] ...
where Z is the subject of WYV and is not controlled by a category containing X.

Now in (88) it is *Bill*, not X (*we each*), which controls PRO. Therefore (89) applies, and EM will be inapplicable to (88). On the other hand, SSC will not apply in the case of (90), so that EM will be allowed.

(90)   We each promised Bill [COMP PRO to kill the other]
         |_____↑

Thus, *we each promised Bill to kill the other* can be converted to *we promised Bill to kill each other*.

3.2. *Counterexamples*

Let us now turn to some problems that arise in connection with TSC, SSC, and Subjacency.

3.2.1. *Clefting*

Clefting provides a new source of counterevidence against successive cyclicity in conjunction with constraint (86). The relevant example is due to Joseph Emonds (personal communication).

(91)   It was in the garage that John put the car.

Note that (91) apparently must involve a transformational operation since the following is ungrammatical.

(92)   *John put the car.

Therefore, (92) apparently derives from a source containing the focus prepositional phrase in the *that*-complement. Plausible deep structures include the following.

(93) a.   It was in the garage [s that John put the car in the garage]
     b.   It was Δ [s that John put the car in the garage]

Now if (93a) is adopted as the underlying source of (91), a deletion transformation will be required, but deletion under identity will violate subjacency, SSC, and TSC in the following example.

(94)   It was in the garage that Mary said that John put the car.

On the other hand, if (93b) is adopted as the underlying source for (91), a movement transformation will be required. Clearly, movement in one sweep from the nonfocus position to Δ will again constitute a violation of subjacency, SSC, and TSC. Consequently, movement must proceed in a successive cyclic fashion. This is illustrated in (95).

(95)

It was Δ [s COMP Mary said [s COMP John put the car [pp in the garage]]]

But this derivation also leads to a violation, since the final movement from the COMP to the focus position entails a violation of (86b). This is so since the PP moves from a COMP position to a nonCOMP position.

3.2.2. *Comparative Subdeletion*

Bresnan [9] has provided additional examples which pose problems for

Subjacency. She argues for a rule of Comparative Subdeletion which deletes underlying measure phrases in examples such as the following.

(96) a. Why were there *more* women on TV than there were ___ men?
  b. There weren't *as many* men on TV as there were ___ women.

This deletion, she argues, violates Subjacency in examples such as the following.

(97) Therefore, they can hire more women than the Administration would allow them to hire ___ men.

Bresnan advances arguments against a movement analysis for such examples. If her arguments against movement are correct, her examples constitute counterevidence to Subjacency.

3.2.3. wh-*Movement*

Chomsky adduces the following examples and assigns them the underlying structures provided in (99).

(98) a. They will obey any request to kill each other.
  b. *They will okay any request to kill each other.
(99) a. They each will obey [any request [COMP PRO to kill the other]]
  b. They each will okay [any request [COMP Δ to kill the other]]

It is assumed that *they each* controls PRO in (99a), but not Δ in (99b). Given the revised SSC (89), PRO will not function as a specified subject in (99a). Therefore EM will be applicable, giving rise to (98a). However, Δ will function as a specified subject under (89) in (99b). Hence EM will not be applicable and (98b) will be blocked.[16]

In this connection consider the following examples in which, following the above reasoning, we would conclude that Δ is present in the structures underlying the examples.

(100) a.*They will okay any proposal to kill each other.
   b. Which Cubans did the White House okay a proposal to kill?
   c. It was Castro that the White House okayed a proposal to assassinate.

Since presumably (100a–c) all contain Δ in their underlying structures, that Δ should function as a specified subject given the revised version of the constraint (89). This leads to the false prediction that (100b, c) are ungrammatical.

3.2.4. Each-*Movement*

Let us return now to EM in connection with examples such as the following.

(101) a. It would be pleasant for the rich for the poor immigrants to do the hard work.
     b. It would be pleasant for each of the men for the poor immigrants to do the hard work.
     c. It would be pleasant for each of the men for the others to do the hard work.
     c. *It would be pleasant for the men for each other to do the hard work.

All of these examples involve a PP+S complement, and it is clear from (101c) that quantified phrases can occupy the PP slot with *the others* functioning as the subject of the embedded S. Chomsky's approach predicts that EM should be applicable to (101c) to yield (101d) since there is no intervening specified subject and no tensed S. Yet (101d) is not grammatical. If, alternatively, EM is viewed as interpretive, as suggested in section 2, there will be nothing to block the relevant interpretation in the case of (101d) since SSC and TSC are not applicable. Examples such as (101d), therefore, appear to constitute evidence against the conditions approach. By contrast, (101d), can be ruled out in a straightforward manner according to the suggestion of section 2.2 that object pronouns not be generated in the subject position of S's.[17]

3.2.5. *Object Shift*

Consider the following examples.

(102) a. It is pleasant for the rich to do the hard work.
     b. The hard work is pleasant for the rich to do.

Example (102b) is perfectly grammatical and yet the deep structure Chomsky assigns to it is the following.

(103)   It is pleasant for the rich [COMP PRO to do the hard work]

Now Chomsky notes that Object Shift should not be applicable given the revised version of SSC as (86). This follows since *it* functions as X, and PRO is not controlled by a category containing X. It is because of this new difficulty that Chomsky reanalyses Object Shift as two rules – PRO-Replacement and It-Replacement – and incorporates traces into his framework. A representative derivation is given in (104).

(104)   It is easy [for PRO to please John]   PRO-Replacement
         It is easy [for John to please]   It-Replacement
         John$_1$ is easy [for t$_1$ to please]

Chomsky argues that this reanalysis does not constitute a complication since It-Replacement is needed in any event to get *John seems to be a nice fellow* according to (105).

(105)   It seems [COMP John to be a nice fellow]   It-Replacement
         John seems to be a nice fellow

Now the claim that such a reanalysis of Object Shift does not constitute a complication in the grammar of English clearly rests on the truth of the claim that It-Replacement can be utilized in the derivation (105). But Chomsky himself notes that this entails complications. Thus, It-Replacement must somehow be blocked in (106).

(106)   It is pleasant for the rich [for the workers to do the work]
         *The workers are pleasant for the rich to do the work

Since *the workers are pleasant for the rich to do the work* is ungrammatical, new machinery is necessary to avoid the bad result. Chomsky's analysis involves stating PRO-Replacement so as to 'combine' the moved object of the complement with PRO and stating It-Replacement so that it is obligatory when (i) PRO is part of the subject complement and when (ii) PRO is not present in structures such as that evidenced in (105). This proposal is contrived inasmuch as PRO-Replacement is the only such rule to 'combine' constituents and inasmuch as the 'independent' motivation for It-Replacement is repossessed in view of the difference in obligatoriness with respect to the related structures and presence of PRO. It should also be added that none of the relevant rules are explicitly formulated.

     Thus, the conclusion would seem to be inescapable, namely that simple Object Shift examples such as (102) are counterevidence to SSC. In this connection, it should be remarked that none of the difficulties discussed here arise in the VP framework discussed in section 2.1.

     Before closing this subsection, I would like to offer one final argument against the foregoing approach to Object Shift. It is well known that arbitrarily long strings of verbs do not block application of this rule. Thus, Bresnan has cited examples such as the following.

(107)   John is hard for Bill to even begin to try to please.

Now, if Chomsky's underlying structures are adopted, then (108) will underlie (107).

(108)   It is hard for Bill [for PRO to even begin [for PRO to try [for PRO to please John]]]

Now if *John* is moved directly and substituted for *it*, not only will this violate SSC, as noted above, but also it will violate subjacency. On the other hand, if the PRO-Replacement analysis is adopted, *John* will 'combine' with the PRO of the innermost embedded S. But now It-Replacement applied to this result will violate subjacency! Thus, new elaborations are needed to derive (107). Presumably PRO-Replacement must apply in a successive cyclic fashion. But apparently this rule 'combines' an object NP with PRO, whereas after one application, it would have to 'combine' a subject instance of an NP/PRO combination with PRO. Without explicit rules, it is difficult to envision what such an analysis would look like, and whether, in fact, it would even be formulable.

3.2.7. *Superiority*

Chomsky attempts to account for the ungrammaticality of the following examples.

(109) a.*John knows what who saw.
      b.*To whom does John know what books to give?

These examples are to be read without echo intonation, for when echo intonation is present the examples are fine. The account of (109) offered in [12] involves a new condition which is called Superiority.

(110)   Superiority: No rule can involve X, Y in the structure
      $\ldots X \ldots [\ldots Z \ldots -WYV \ldots] \ldots$
      where the rule applies ambiguously to Z and Y and Z is superior to Y.

Consider how this condition predicts the ungrammaticality of (109b). Here the COMP of the underlying matrix clause functions as the X of (86). The rule of *wh*-fronting would apply ambiguously to *what books*, which is Z, and to *to whom*, which is Y. But Z is superior to Y, so (109b) constitutes a violation of (110). By contrast, *What books does John know to give to whom*, in which case Z is moved, does not constitute a violation and is indeed grammatical.

The following examples are counterexamples to Superiority.

(111) a. What books does John want which student to read?
      b. What books does John want who else to read?

To my ear such examples are quite natural when read without echo intonation.

4. Conclusion

In section 2, the evidence adduced to support TSC and SSC has been assessed, and alternatives have been suggested which adequately account for the relevant range of data. In some cases, it has been argued that the alternatives provide a more general account than the constraints. Additional counterexamples to SSC and TSC have been provided in section 3, and Subjacency and Superiority were also criticized.

In this paper, I have confined my remarks to Chomsky's original paper [12]. In recent works [13, 14], traces have assumed a more prominent role than in the original essay. Constraints such as TSC and SSC are now interpreted as constraints on surface structures, a move which is made possible by the fact that traces serve to code into surface structures all relevant aspects of the earlier transformational history of moved phrases. Now clearly, trace theory and constraints such as TSC and SSC are logically independent. Nevertheless, a good deal of the plausibility for trace theory is intimately bound up with the plausibility of TSC and SSC, since, in practice, it is constraints such as these that are now taken to be "conditions on an enriched surface structure involving traces, instead of conditions on the application of rules" [14:317]. In light of the criticism that can be leveled against TSC and SSC, it may be appropriate now to rethink the feasibility of trace theory itself.

NOTES

[1] See, for example, [14].

[2] A number of relevant papers have appeared too late for discussion here: critical essays by Yagi [26], Ikeuchi [20], and Bach/Horn [1] for example, as well as Chomsky's most recent contribution [15], which further refines and revises the proposals appraised here.

[3] Actually the treatment of Object Shift presented here reflects Chomsky's initial formulation. At a later point in the development of his conditions he reanalyzes Object Shift as two processes, thus obviating some of the initial development. The reanalysis is discussed below in subsection 3.2.5.

[4] Rule (10) can be extended in the obvious way to allow *this violin would be easy to play the Kreuzer sonata on.*

[5] A somewhat different analysis of Object Shift cases which is consistent with Bresnan's VP hypothesis is offered in [3]. Cf. also the exchange between Bresnan and Berman/Szamosi, which is discussed in [2].

[6] Chomsky and Dougherty differ in important respects. Dougherty converts *each of the candidates hated the other* into *the candidates hated each other* by means of three distinct transformations – Quantifier Postposition, Quantifier Movement, and *each other*-Transformation. Dougherty provides an explicit formulation of all three rules. Chomsky apparently accepts a version of Dougherty's Quantifier Postposition while the distinction between Quantifier Movement and *each other*-Transformation is blurred. These rules are not stated, and it is therefore difficult to determine precisely to what extent Dougherty's analysis is followed.

[7] One basic objection to the movement approach to *each other* has been voiced by Postal, who

cited *the men talked to each other about each other* as underivable under the movement assumption since the subject could give rise to only a single instance of *each*, cf. [24:72]. Additional arguments against movement are provided in Fiengo and Lasnik [18] and Brame [4]. In the latter it is shown that the putative arguments for movement are in fact strong arguments against it. Additional arguments against movement are also provided, including arguments against the Quantifier Postposition transformation that is accepted by Fiengo and Lasnik.

[8] An obvious argument against movement here is the fact that reciprocals such as *one another* behave similarly, viz. *the boys think that Bill will fool one another*, where there is no candidate for movement such as *each*. See Brame [4] for additional examples.

[9] Apparent counterexamples are discussed in [6].

[10] Here, as elsewhere in this paper, subscripts are utilized as a formal device to distinguish distinct occurrences of syntactic units, not as an indication of intended reference.

[11] For more on the distinction, cf. Hust and Brame [19] and Lasnik [22].

[12] I am following Chomsky [10] in assuming that *John's* is the subject of the NP construction.

[13] A similar point is made in a somewhat different context by Bresnan [8:46].

[14] The idioms differ from the *until* phrase in exhibiting full grammaticality in 'affective' contexts.

   (i) a. Do you give a damn about your exam?
      b. Does it cut any ice whether you pass?
      c. *Will you leave until midnight?
  (ii) a. If you give a damn, you'll pass that exam.
      b. If it cuts any ice, he'll tell us.
      c. *If he leaves until midnight, he'll tell us.

[15] Excluding the "... at all" reading which is often possible in nonaffective contexts.

[16] Throughout his paper, Chomsky assumes a notion of control which is never made explicit, citing Jackendoff [21] for clarification. But Jackendoff here provides no explicit analysis of how control is assigned; cf. [19] for discussion. It seems that some of the problems raised might resolve themselves automatically if control were made explicit. Control appears to be simply a name for a problem; its resolution involves taking seriously a program for working out Equi within an interpretive framework. See [3] for one proposal.

[17] In earlier sections, I spoke of the restriction as one related to tensed S's, but the more general formulation is needed in view of examples such as (101d). If correct, this shows that reciprocal pronouns such as *each other* are not part of S complements in examples such as *They expect each other to win*. Thus, the evidence argues against Chomsky's anti-raising position; cf. [12]. However, as I have argued in [4], there is no rule of Raising as classically conceived. Thus, I take a position intermediate between Chomsky on the one hand, who argues against Raising but fails to adopt the correct surface structures, and Postal on the other, who adopts the correct surface structures, but fails to recognize that such structures are identical to the base structures, i.e. that Raising does not exist. Cf. [4] for detailed discussion.

REFERENCES

[1] Bach, E. and Horn, G. M.: 1976, 'Remarks on "Conditions on Transformations"', *Linguistic Inquiry* **7**, 265–299.

[2] Brame, M. K.: 1975, 'The VP Controversy', *Linguistic Analysis* **1**, 191–203.

[3] Brame, M. K.: 1976, *Conjectures and Refutations in Syntax and Semantics*, North-Holland Publishing Co.

[4] Brame, M. K.: 1976, 'Quantifiers, Reciprocals, and Raising', unpublished ms.

[5] Brame, M. K.: 1977, 'The Base Hypothesis and the Spelling Prohibition', unpublished paper delivered at the Eighth Annual Colloquium on Directions in Linguistics, University of Calgary, March 21, 1977.

[6] Brame, M. K.: 1977, 'Scope Phenomena', to appear.

[7] Bresnan, J. W. 1971. 'Sentence Stress and Syntactic Transformations', *Language* **47**, 257–81. Reprinted in *Contributions to Generative Phonology*, M. K. Brame, ed. Austin, Tex.: University of Texas Press.

[8] Bresnan, J.: 1975, 'Comparative Deletion and Constraints on Transformations', *Linguistic Analysis* **1**, 25–74.

[9] Bresnan, J.: 1976, 'Evidence for a Theory of Unbounded Transformations', *Linguistic Analysis* **2**, 353–393.

[10] Chomsky, N.: 1970, 'Remarks on Nominalization', in *Readings in English Transformational Grammar*, R. A. Jacobs and P. S. Rosenbaum, eds. Waltham, Mass.: Ginn. Reprinted in *Studies on Semantics in Generative Grammar*, N. Chomsky, 1972. The Hague: Mouton.

[11] Chomsky, N.: 1972, 'Some Empirical Issues in the Theory of Transformational Grammar', In *Goals of Linguistic Theory*, S. Peters, ed., 1972. Englewood Cliffs, N.J.: Prentice-Hall. Reprinted in *Studies on Semantics in Generative Grammar*, N. Chomsky, 1972. The Hague: Mouton.

[12] Chomsky, N.: 1973, 'Conditions on Transformations', in *A Festschrift for Morris Halle*, S. R. Anderson and P. Kiparsky, eds. New York: Holt, Rinehart, and Winston.

[13] Chomsky, N.: 1975, *Reflections on Language*. New York: Pantheon Books.

[14] Chomsky, N.: 1976, 'Conditions on Rules of Grammar', *Linguistic Analysis* **2**, 303–351.

[15] Chomsky, N.: 1976, 'On *wh*-Movement', paper presented at the Conference on Formal Syntax, June 1976, University of California at Irvine.

[16] Dougherty, R. C.: 1970, 'A Grammar of Coordinate Conjoined Structures I', *Language* **46**, 850–98.

[17] Emonds, J. E.: 1976, *A Transformational Approach to English Syntax: Root, Structure-Preserving, and Local Transformations*. New York: Academic Press, Inc.

[18] Fiengo, R. and Lasnik, H.: (1973), 'The Logical Structure of Reciprocal Sentences in English', *Foundations of Language* **9**, 447–468.

[19] Hust, J. R. and Brame, M. K. 1976, 'Jackendoff on Interpretive Semantics: A Review of *Semantic Interpretation in Generative Grammar* by R. Jackendoff', *Linguistic Analysis* **2**, 243–277.

[20] Ikeuchi, N.: 1976, 'Notes on the New Subjacency Condition', *Studies in English Linguistics* **4**, 139–142.

[21] Jackendoff, R. S.: 1972, *Semantic Interpretation in Generative Grammar*. Cambridge, Mass.: MIT Press.

[22] Lasnik, H.: 1976, 'Remarks on Coreference', *Linguistic Analysis* **2**; 1–22.

[23] Lees, R. B.: 1960, 'A Multiply Ambiguous Adjective Construction in English', *Language* **36**, 204–21.

[24] Postal, P. M.: 1974, *On Raising*. Cambridge, Mass.: MIT Press.

[25] van Riemsdijk, H. 1975. 'Extraction from PP and the Head Constraint', to appear in *Linguistic Analysis*.

[26] Yagi, T.: 1976, 'Review of "Conditions on Transformations" by N. Chomsky', *Studies in English Linguistics* **4**, 112–137.